Reading Song Lyrics

Reading Song Lyrics

An Interdisciplinary and Multimodal Approach

Glenn Fosbraey

ANTHEM PRESS

Anthem Press
An imprint of Wimbledon Publishing Company
www.anthempress.com

This edition first published in UK and USA 2025
by ANTHEM PRESS
75–76 Blackfriars Road, London SE1 8HA, UK
or PO Box 9779, London SW19 7ZG, UK
and
244 Madison Ave #116, New York, NY 10016, USA

© 2025 Glenn Fosbraey

The author asserts the moral right to be identified as the author of this work.

All rights reserved. Without limiting the rights under copyright reserved above, no part of this publication may be reproduced, stored or introduced into a retrieval system, or transmitted, in any form or by any means (electronic, mechanical, photocopying, recording or otherwise), without the prior written permission of both the copyright owner and the above publisher of this book.

British Library Cataloguing-in-Publication Data
A catalogue record for this book is available from the British Library.

Library of Congress Cataloging-in-Publication Data: 2025934727
A catalog record for this book has been requested.

ISBN-13: 978-1-83999-500-2 (Pbk)
ISBN-10: 1-83999-500-9 (Pbk)

Credit: PixelAnarchy, Reisen, Fotographie, Sport

This title is also available as an e-book.

CONTENTS

1. Introduction   1
2. Inside the song: Constructing 'meaning'   9
3. Going Outside   43
4. Conclusion   61

References   63

Chapter 1

INTRODUCTION

1. Discussing Popular Music Studies as an Academic Discipline

The primary aim of my work in the field of popular music studies so far has been to recognise popular music as a multimodal form and an academic field worthy of the same considerations historically afforded to literature, film, or drama. For the analysis of all of song's components, my research has required an interdisciplinary approach, where I have drawn upon, for example, new criticism, narratology, gender studies, sociological theory, psychoanalysis, critical race theory, feminist theory, historicism, and a range of theories related to the fields of film and media studies in order to properly analyse the visual materials that often accompany song. In my chapter 'I'm (not) your man: Reading Leonard Cohen's Lyrics without Leonard Cohen' (Fosbraey, 2017: 57–69), I conclude by saying that if ever song lyrics are to be appreciated in an academic environment the way that other subjects are, then they need to be analysed using similar rigorous critical theories. I have used this as a further objective within my work to date, and it will be central to the work I will undertake in the future. In my research, however far away from the song itself I appear to move, I maintain a link back to the lyrics, keeping them front and centre in all discussions and observing to what extent the multimodal and external factors such as author biography, album art, music video, and social media engagement impact how we might react to them. And while the *sound* of songs is obviously key, I tend to focus on it in a way that, once again, focuses on the lyrics, using the vocal melodies, harmonies (including counter-melodies), instrumentation, and production as another way of showing how our reaction to the lyrics can be influenced by factors outside the words themselves. Any theory-heavy musicological analysis is therefore absent from my work as it presents itself as a closed system that is resistant to any outside discussion (including lyrics), and my writing demonstrates that, if we are to legitimise popular song as an area of academic study and scholarship, it needs also to be accessible to those from other disciplines.

With regard to song lyrics specifically, although a group of scholars have succeeded in drawing attention to them as a serious art form worthy of academic consideration, their work has also brought with it a set of problems. The title of Eckstein's 2010 *Reading Song Lyrics* suggests it might be an entire full-length text that critically analyses popular music lyrics, as does his assertion towards the beginning that 'lyrics are not poetry, and their study therefore requires a different set of analytical tools from that which is conventionally applied to poetry' (Eckstein, 2010: 23). But although he does point to the importance of 'mediality of language [...] style and musical context [...], social embeddedness and cultural value, and [...] an understanding of the reciprocal relationship between (embodied) verbal input and performance ideology' (Eckstein, 2010: 38), Eckstein does not apply these 'tools' to *modern* popular music, instead concerning himself with sixteenth- to eighteenth-century ballads, including more than eighty pages exploring different versions of 'Scarborough Fair'. Other texts have included additional elements alongside lyrical analysis, as Powell (2010) does in *How Music Works* looking at popular music studies from a musicological perspective. But, as is often the case where musicology is introduced, although Powell (2010) aims to 'keep the style conversational' and demonstrate that 'music can be understood on a very fundamental level' (Powell, 2010: 4), *How Music Works* consistently deploys language and terminology that can only be understood by musicologists (e.g., using a diagram of relative string length versus relative frequency on the Harp to discuss 'leading' and 'closest relative' notes within 'the original pentatonic set' in a conversation about emotion). Bicknell's attempts to explain emotional connection with popular music in her book *Why Music Moves Us* are equally inaccessible to the non-musicologist, speaking of 'a specific association between trance states and a certain tonal pattern – the Phrygian mode' (Bicknell, 2009: 63). What I have done in my own work is to combine detailed lyrical analysis that makes clear the 'tools' I am using, but to also expand the discussion into the fields of sociology, psychoanalysis, and visual media.

In their 2002 edited collection *Popular Music Studies*, Hesmondhalgh and Negus classified the area of popular music studies as 'uniquely interdisciplinary', which draws upon 'significant contributions from writers within a number of academic fields, including musicology, media and cultural studies, sociology, anthropology, ethnomusicology, folklorists, psychology, social history and cultural geography' (Hesmondhalgh & Negus, 2002: 1). Although this is helpful in demonstrating the breadth of work that the area encompasses, what they are actually describing is *multi*disciplinary rather than *inter*disciplinary, and it has, perhaps, been this multifaceted nature of analysis that has created problems with popular music studies to date (and in particular the analysis of popular music lyrics), with critics trying to position their works within existing fields instead of treating popular music as a field worthy of its own set of considerations. Way and McKerrell's 2017 edited collection *Music as Multimodal Discourse: Semiotics, Power and Protest* gets the closest to what I want to achieve with this book when they consider music as a multimodal communication, but they work on 'examining the interacting meaning potential of sonic aspects such as rhythm, instrumentation, pitch, tonality, melody and their interrelationships with text, image and other modes' (Bloomsbury, 2017), thus positioning at least part of itself under the musicological analysis umbrella, with other parts focusing on the broader (i.e., not at the individual song level) impact of popular song, such as the chapters 'Recontextualization and Fascist Music', 'On the Interplay of Music, Voice and Lyrics in the Advertising Jingle', and 'Articulations in Protest Music Videos' Struggle with Countercultural Politics and Authenticity'.

The title of Eckstein's 2010 *Reading Song Lyrics* suggests that it might be an entire full-length text that critically analyses popular music lyrics, as does his assertion towards the beginning that 'lyrics are not poetry, and their study therefore requires a different set of analytical tools from that which is conventionally applied to poetry' (Eckstein, 2010: 23). But although he does point to the importance of 'mediality of language [...] style and musical context [...], social embeddedness and cultural value, and [...] an understanding of the reciprocal relationship between (embodied) verbal input and performance ideology' (Eckstein, 2010: 38), Eckstein does not apply these 'tools' to *modern* popular music, instead concerning himself with sixteenth- to eighteenth-century ballads, including more than eighty pages exploring different versions of 'Scarborough Fair'. So, although it is undoubtedly an important contribution to understanding popular song of the sixteenth to eighteenth centuries, the book does not offer too much in terms of what I seek to explore in my own work that focuses on reading twentieth- and twenty-first-century songs.

2. Approaching Song Lyrics as Poetry: The Importance and Limitations of This Approach

Although the critic Christopher Ricks refers to Bob Dylan as a 'poet' as far back as 1974 in his book *Keats and Embarrassment*, it is via his 2004 book *Dylan's Visions of Sin* that he solidifies this assertion, where he constantly refers to Bob Dylan's lyrics as 'poetry' and compares his work with other poets. Ricks does concede that 'songs are different from poems' but then focuses on their main difference being songs' performative elements before returning to what seems to be his main aim of the book when he asks 'is Dylan a poet?' and conducting a compare and contrast exercise between the lyrics of 'Highway 61 Revisited' and Philip Larkin's 'Love Songs In Age'. In his chapter 'Songs, Poems, Rhymes', Ricks spends thirty-seven pages discussing the performativity of songs (including the effect of re-performance), cadences, voicing, and what he calls 'rhymical draping', and accepts that song is a mixed-media art form but significantly fails to determine what he thinks the differences are between *spoken word* poetry and song, both of which share performative elements. Comparing lyrics that, by definition, are 'words sung to a tune' (Collins Dictionary) and 'whose full effect depends upon music' (Rooksby, 2006: 96) with written poems that appear without a performed element in books or pamphlets seems forced and unhelpful, like comparing a photograph with a film. In his paper 'The Poetry of Bob Dylan' at the University of Richmond in 2011, Ricks does attempt to identify the difference between poetry and song (once again, though, *written* poetry), saying that 'the key differentiation […] is that song can use melisma', which he defines as 'the flowering of one note into several syllables' (Ricks, 2011). Certainly, melisma is a component of song, but to cite it as the *key* difference between the two forms is to ignore several crucial components. It ignores, for example, how the instrumentation and arrangement can impact upon what we take from the lyrics in terms of meaning, context, or subtext (Rojek, 2011: 183) (see The Baseballs' version of 'Umbrella' and then compare that to Rihanna's version), or how the melody affects our emotional connection to the lyrics (Juslin & Sloboda, 2001) (see Devo's version of '(I Can't Get No) Satisfaction and then compare that to The Rolling Stones' version). I discuss this in my book *Reading Eminem*, suggesting that

> the similarities between hip hop lyrics and poetry shouldn't be ignored and rhythm and rhyme, use of simile and metaphor, and use of storytelling are certainly vital to both forms […but] in the case of Eminem, to focus only on his lyrics […] glosses over the importance of the melodic hook in his songs, or the use of sampling, and production. (Fosbraey, 2022b: 3)

As Rooksby observes, 'a lyric is a set of words intended to be sung, and to be supported by music' (Rooksby, 2006: 96) and to isolate the lyrics from their natural environment is to analyse only 'one half of a work' (Gottlieb & Kimbal, 2000: xxiv) or, as Jarvis Cocker puts it, 'like watching the TV with the sound turned down; you're only really getting half the story' (Cocker, 2011: 2). It also ignores the performative elements of song, such as voice, which John Lydon identifies as being key to the transference of 'message'.

As he says: 'I use the line in "Rise" the written word is a lie, because it generally is without the human tone on it; the double entendres just by inflections; the irony just by a mannerism in a tone is vital to the bigger picture' (Rachel, 2013: 145).

In his paper 'Music of Poetry and Poetry of Song: Expressivity and Grammar in Vocal Performance', Tyler Bickford analyses Dylan's song 'Down the Highway' *as* a song, identifying the linguistic and grammatical elements of the lyrics but also focusing on his 'idiosyncratic' singing style, which 'highlights the pronunciation and inflection of words and phrases [...] places irregular stress on words [... and] often sees him pronounce [...] lyrics in unexpected ways [...] with short vowels and plosive stops' (Bickford, 2007: 446–451). 'An analysis that does not account for the containment of music and poetry within the domain of the voice', Bickford notes, 'misses a remarkably clear example of a distinctly musico-poetic progression that builds large formal structures out of tiny musical and poetic elements' (Bickford, 2007: 462–463). The tendency to divorce the lyrics from their musical setting is not a process used solely by Ricks, however, and is perhaps taken to its extreme with lyric collections such as *Nick Cave: The Complete Lyrics, 1978–2013; Paul Simon: Lyrics 1964–2011* (2008); *Bob Dylan: 1962–2001 Lyrics* (2016); *Bruce Springsteen Like a Killer in the Sun: Selected Lyrics 1972–2017*; and *Paul McCartney: The Lyrics 1956 – the present* (2021). Simkin observes that 'both Dylan and Springsteen have had their lyrics published more than once each as collections akin to books of poetry, even though both have questioned in interview the value of divorcing the words from their music.' (Simkin, 2020: 15). Such processes, however, are nothing new. In his 2007 book *Pop Music and Society*, Longhurst observed that 'early attempts to study pop music [...] often considered the lyrics as a form of poetry, suggesting that certain pop writers could be seen as poets' (Longhurst, 2007: 158). Goldstein's *Poetry of Rock* began this trend, comparing songs to other media in an attempt to give them 'high culture legitimacy' (Astor, 2010: 143). With questions such as 'Is John Lennon's wordplay truly Joycean?' and 'Is Bob Dylan the Walt Whitman of the jukebox?', as well as comparing 'The Silhouettes' 'Get a Job' with concrete poetry and The Jaynetts' 'Sally, Go Round the Roses' with Waiting for Godot' (Astor, 2010: 143), Goldstein is concerned more with placing song alongside literature, poetry, and drama than he is with actually seeing it as a unique art form and analysing it accordingly.

In a 2023 newspaper article, 'world expert on William Shakespeare' Sir Jonathan Bate situates himself as a latter-day Ricks with his assertion that 'lyricists are poets', comparing Taylor Swift to 'some of history's greatest writers – including the Bard himself' and describing her as a 'real poet'

(Harrison, 2023) not 'just' a pop music lyricist. Beyond this clickbait-like statement, the main thrust of Bate's article is the rather obvious observation that there are parallels between Swift's 2010 song 'Love Story' and Shakespeare's *Romeo and Juliet*, and he goes on to speak of Emily Dickinson, Robert Frost, Charlotte Bronte, and William Wordsworth in a rather desperate attempt to 'compare her (favourably) to the giants of literature' (Bate, 2023). When it comes to actually looking *at* the song 'Love Story' rather than at its influences, inspirations, or allusions, Bate is only able to offer a rather brief review, rather than critique, saying as he does that 'Love Story, is an 'almost perfect pop song, with its catchy hook, driving rhythm and ingenious use of banjo and mandolin' (Bate, 2023). All the article succeeds in doing is to say that it is comparisons to writers outside the medium of song lyrics that makes Swift 'clever' (and yes, he does use this word). Such analyses ignore the way songwriters can utilise the medium of song to distil complex modern concerns into a few lines, all while attaching the words to simple, effective, and memorable vocal melodies (in Swift's case, see 'You need to calm down'), endear themselves to their fans by referring to their own life experiences to show vulnerability and self-deprecation (in Swift's case, see pretty much any song from *1989*), or take on the personae of various characters to create a range of narrative threads (with regard to Swift, see the albums *Folklore* and *Evermore*). As Levitin says: 'the shape of lyrics is influenced by different things than the shape of poetry – the melody and rhythms of music provide an extrinsic framework, whereas poetry's structure is intrinsic' (Levitin, 2008a: 23). Comparing the two, therefore, is not the compliment Bate intends it to be. As Leith notes, it does not elevate lyrics to call them poetry 'any more than it elevates an apple to call it an orange; nor does it give you a useful way of thinking about it academically' (Leith, 2007).

3. Defining the 'Text'

If we are to analyse popular song seriously, one of the first things we must do is decide which components we consider to be the 'text'. Shuker says that 'to study popular music is to study popular culture [... although] much writing on popular music tends to treat it in isolation from the literature in the general field within which it is situated' (Shuker, 1997: 1). Although this is helpful in underlining the importance of drawing on a breadth of information to conduct a considered analysis of popular music, it is somewhat problematic in that it is offering the critic an excuse to look, as Hopps (2009: 9) says, 'through' rather than 'at' the songs themselves. Although the process of viewing lyrics as poetry is also problematic as it isolates the words from the rest of the song and therefore gives us only a partial picture of the complete text, it is useful, at least, in making critics pay attention to a song's contents.

In *Writing Song Lyrics: Creative and Critical approaches*, I outline the need to expand and explicitly define what we see as the 'text' when discussing and analysing popular music. 'In a novel', I suggest,

> we can see what the text is: whatever appears within the pages, perhaps including the front and back covers, blurb and author biography if applicable, but the text is defined as the words of the novel itself. Everything is contained in the words, sentences, paragraphs, chapters and so on that make up the pages of the novel. The same is true for a poem. (Fosbraey & Melrose, 2019: 3)

With a song, however, there are other factors to consider. The song is a combination of music and lyric, both of which can be read as well as heard; and then there is the accompanying material that surrounds the delivery. Although we could certainly make the argument that visual elements can also have a significant impact on our reading of other formats (for example, the jackets of novels), album covers and the music contained within 'can be linked so intensely that it is hard to decide where one begins and the other ends' (Draper, 2008: 13). So, when we are defining the 'text', should the 'text' include cover art, information found inside the sleeve or booklet, including lyric transcriptions (for hard copy) or website (for download/streaming)? Should 'text' include music video? And to what extent should we allow these factors to influence our readings of the songs?' (Fosbraey & Melrose, 2019: 3). I decided that the minimum the 'text' could be is what comes 'out of speakers or headphones, without any other factors interfering with the experience' (Fosbraey & Melrose, 2019: 3). 'Even if the artist published the lyrics in the album sleeve, anything that can't be heard or understood from listening, involves research beyond the song itself, and the physical reading of the lyrics, rather than listening to them, is to hunt for clarity and/or meaning, and the first step that many people may take to start analysing a text by distancing themselves from what is actually there' (Fosbraey, 2017: 61).

From this starting point of defining the parameters we are working within when it comes to analysing popular song, it became possible to identify a relatively simple but highly suggestive dual framework of analysis, grounded in the experience of listening. In *Writing Song Lyrics*, I labelled these frameworks 'staying inside the song' and anything beyond this (including album art, music video, artist biography, and interviews) 'going *outside* the song'. This approach enabled me to combine the two approaches to form a more detailed, thorough analysis of single songs, with the 'inside' technique allowing for different reading practices to be acknowledged, employed, and discussed, and the 'outside' technique allowing us to observe the impact external factors such as society, politics, and accompanying visual materials have on how we interpret the songs. In doing so, I bring together what have previously been two discrete approaches to analysis to formulate a new interdisciplinary and multimodal approach to the field, which I will explore in the following chapters.

Chapter 2

INSIDE THE SONG: CONSTRUCTING 'MEANING'

2.1. Fact or Fiction?

Although the process of viewing lyrics as poetry is problematic, it does at least require critics to look *at* them, rather than straight *through* them to the songwriter's biography. Hopps notes that it's commonplace for critics and fans alike to read lyrics literally, as transparent disclosures of the singer's biography (Hopps, 2009: 9), and David Byrne agrees, noting that the assumption is that 'everything one sings emerges from some autobiographical impulse' (Byrne, 2012: 155). Such methods of 'analysis' are a staple of album and single reviews, but they also regularly feature in academic texts, for example (to cite but a few) Timothy Taylor's chapter on the song 'Johnny B. Goode', where he focuses on the 'meanings' of the lyrics, and frequently debates which lyrics have an 'autobiographical nature' (Taylor, 2000: 167); in William Echard's book *Neil Young and the Poetics of Energy* where he links Young's portrayal of 'masculine-coded properties' in his lyrics back to his personal life (Echard, 2005: 19); and in Keith Clifton's chapter, 'Queer hearing and the Madonna Queen' where he attaches the lyrics of 'Papa Don't Preach' to the singer's relationship with her father). Our desire to, as Hopps says, treat lyrics 'as a sort of stethoscope [...] and read unproblematically backwards from text to the "heart and soul" of the author' (Hopps, 2009: 85), is indicative of our obsession with viewing lyrics as ciphers and their authors as the encryption keys, which in turn leads us towards their biographies to find out as much about them as we can. The more we know, the more likely we are to crack the cipher, after all. I write in *Writing Song Lyrics* about how I always start my Level 5 lyric writing classes with the Beatles song 'Yesterday' to demonstrate how our knowledge of the artists themselves can affect the way we receive a song. Playing, first of all, an instrumental version of 'Yesterday' to explore how melody alone can achieve an emotional response (the reaction usually sees the students describing it in variations of the term 'bittersweet', mixing 'sad' and 'happy' emotions), I then play a version of the song where I got a singer friend of mine to use the draft lyrics Paul McCartney initially attached to the melody, with its working title 'Scrambled Eggs'. This demonstrates how lyrics can influence our reactions to a melody, as many of the students are distracted by the nonsensical words, losing any of their initial reactions to the melody alone. Next, I play the Beatles' version as it appeared on the Help album in the UK, and as a single release in the US. I note in *Writing Song Lyrics* that I put at least part of the success of the song down to 'the sheer accessibility of the lyrics [...which are] generic enough to be applied to most people's lives if they've experienced any kind of loss, heartbreak, or setback. It doesn't matter if it's not the kind of scenario McCartney was thinking of when he wrote it; it's open to the listeners listener to apply their own experience and thus their own emotion.' (Fosbraey & Melrose, 2019: 71–72). Finally, I give the class some information about McCartney's relationship with the lyrics where a number of writers have put forward the theory that the song focuses on the death of his mother. Although McCartney himself has denied doing this consciously, for the purposes of the exercise it is irrelevant, as the idea has now been put into the students' heads, and 'this research, uncovering as it does McCartney's personal experience with loss, make us believe what he's saying (they're not just empty words now; they have significance and gravitas), and, as we are now more invested in the singer of the song, our emotional attachment lifts again, as we now feel emotion for McCartney, and for ourselves with our own thoughts on loss, heartbreak, or remorse now established' (Fosbraey & Melrose, 2019: 72). And, if we are listening to songs by our favourite artists, we are naturally drawn to obtaining the information that connects us with their lyrics in this way. I note in my journal article 'Disrupting Status Quo: Pedagogical Approaches to Song Lyrics' how 'the desire to discover more about an artist is nothing new [...] with fan clubs and band newsletters having been around for decades' (Fosbraey, 2015: 59–60), but with more and more artists releasing autobiographies, websites like Wikipedia and Biography.com, and artists' own online presence via social media platforms, it's never been easier to find information.

 With an artist like Eminem, who keeps his private life from the public glare, shuns social media and does not engage in many interviews with the media, the temptation for fans and critics alike is to use his lyrics as the primary source to get that personal information they seek. Eminem complains about such behaviour as 'overanalysing' (Eminem, 2000), but it is, in fact, a classic case of underanalysing, where the work itself is largely ignored, used only as a conduit to the author, leading numerous critics to busy themselves with trying to figure out an answer to the question: 'who is Eminem, who is Marshall, who is Slim Shady?' I respond to this in *Reading Eminem*, suggesting that they are all characters in the same fashion as David Bowie's Ziggy

Stardust, Aladdin Sane, Halloween Jack, and The Think White Duke, but with Eminem, he does his 'dressing up' internally through his lyrics, 'editing himself into different characters and giving them different voices in record, despite them looking the same in his album artwork, publicity shots, and music videos. Less obviously, perhaps, Marshall Mathers the songwriter has also invented Marshall Mathers the character for his lyrics, a character who should be looked upon as fictious as Slim Shady and Eminem' (Fosbraey, 2022b: 86–87).

The presumed fictional status of both character and narrative is common in media other than lyrics, where novelists, screenwriters, and playwrights alike are presumed to have created their content from their imaginations rather than personal experience, even when writing in the first person. As French Historian Michael Foucault says 'everyone knows that, in a novel offered as a narrator's account, neither the first-person pronoun nor the present indicative refers exactly to the writer or to the moment in which he writes but, rather, to an alter ego whose distance from the author varies' (Braun, 2008: 34). Indeed, we don't find people leaping to the conclusion that Patrick Bateman is a window into the soul of Bret Easton Ellis, that every word Willy Loman utters is a reflection of Arthur Miller, or that Walter White is merely a caricature of his creator Vince Gilligan.

The process of attaching lyrics to their songwriters brings about several problems, not least the concept of 'truth'.

2.1.1. Truth?

As well as fans and critics assuming songs represent a pure outpouring of truth from the lyricist, some artists (and/or their marketing teams) also push the notion of 'lyrics as confession' when promoting their latest work, obviously noting the benefits of allowing their fans to gain insight into their personal lives. Recently, for example, Rita Ora's social media content for her 2023 album *You and I* saw her enthusiastically describing the 'honesty' of her lyrics, which, she says function as 'a diary of the last few years' and detail her 'journey' (MyIrea, 2023). Although this would certainly fit with Wayne Booth's observation that 'true artists, we have been told again and again, take no thought of their readers. They write for themselves […] and let the reader be damned' (Booth, 1961: 89), I argue that 'never has this been less the case with an artist who knows their music is going to be heard by millions. Of course they are writing with the reader in mind, even if they're doing so subconsciously' (Fosbraey & Melrose, 2019: 76). Hopps goes even further proposing that 'all art […] including that which affects to speak most directly and in the most heartfelt way, is a matter of contrivance and manipulation'

(Hopps, 2009: 84). It's a statement that has alarmed many of my students over the years, and the words 'contrivance' and 'manipulation' do sound overly negative, as if artists everywhere are rubbing their hands with glee at the thought of duping their gullible audience once more. But, if we replace them with, say 'creativity' and 'invention', it softens the blow somewhat and gives us the same (well, similar) meaning. Lyrics, coming under the generic 'art' umbrella as they do, have always treated truth as plastic, as something which is susceptible to change based on the needs of the song. This doesn't mean that lyricists lack authenticity or credibility, it just means that they are working within a format which (usually) contains factors which limit the possibility of absolute 'truth'. The biggest factor of all is editing. A songwriter may start with a specific, factual story they want to tell, but in order to make the song appealing and accessible to a mass audience, it's likely it will need to be cut, amended, and manipulated to adhere to various songwriting conventions such as length, structure, rhyme, and rhythm.

In terms of length, songwriter Jimmy Webb notes that lyricists 'must accomplish our aims and tell our entire story in a time frame of about three minutes. This means among other things that we are not vouchsafed the luxury that some of our literary cousins have [...including an] exploration of plot in counterpoint throughout a seamless and climactic story line...' (Webb, 1998: 37) and critics Dolley & Walford say that a song, 'has no time in which to develop character and situations [...and] characters must be flashed on the audience [...] like figures passing a window' (Dolley & Walford, 2015: 3). The notion of the '3 minute pop song' is a generalisation, of course, and there are extremes, with 'Shri Ramcharitmanas' by Dr. Jagdish Pillai at the one end, which has a running time of 138 hours, 41 minutes, and 20 seconds (Ryan, 2024) and contains 116,000 words, and 'You Suffer' by Napalm Death at the other, with a running time of 1.316 seconds and only four words (Randall, 2024) but the 'average length of a pop song has stayed set at between three and four minutes for the last fifty years or so' (Longdon, 2018). A songwriter wishing to write autobiographically within this average won't ever be able to tell the complete truth, purely because the running time won't allow it. Even when a writer wishes to extend their autobiographical explorations beyond the song onto an entire album, or, in the case of Eels' 2005 *Blinking Lights and Other Revelations* a 'double' album, economy of truth is still a requirement. The Eels band website describes *Blinking Lights and Other Revelations* as 'fearlessly autobiographical' (Eels, 2024), and website PopMatters agrees, declaring it 'an autobiographical 33-song masterpiece [... that] even unfolds in chronological order [...and] is meant as a reflection of E's entire life up to this point (PopMatters Staff, 2005). Indeed, its songs are full of seemingly confessional narratives, all told in the first-person perspective, which means the temptation (as we've discussed) is automatically to attach the lyrics squarely to Everett's own life. But, even though *Blinking Lights* [...] has a relatively long running time for an album at ninety-three minutes, if we compare it to the five-hour audiobook running time of Everett's autobiography *Things The Grandchildren Should Know* (which, compared to other such works is on the short side) we can immediately see that, at best *Blinking Lights* [...] is offering less than a third of his actual autobiography, which would have been through several editing processes itself, first via Everett picking and choosing which stories he wants to share, and then via the editing team at Abacus publishers.

The limitations length places on song format may prevent the complete conveyance of truth, but it does encourage a conciseness of expression which can be a real asset to the writer. As Will Self says, Morrissey 'is responsible – among other things – for encapsulating 200 years of philosophical speculation in a single line: "Does the body rule the mind or does the mind rule the body, I dunno"' (Self, 2011: 165), and distilling complex ideas into a short time frame can enhance accessibility, especially in today's world, where information is often digested via short online video clips. As I write in my chapter 'Truth and Manipulation in Pink Floyd's The Final Cut', the condensing of bigger themes into ththree-minute song functions as an 'overview; a news bulletin instead of a Panorama special edition [...which gives] the listener an emotional feel for a situation, rather than detailing the specifics [providing...] maximum impact and maximum understanding' (Fosbraey, 2022a: 387). The brevity of the lyrical format means that lyricists employ a number of 'shortcuts' in order to make the most of the words they *do* have available to them, and in Eminem's case, he often employs what Botha calls 'a "field of familiar signs" – generic characters and situations, historically and culturally specific events or objects – which act as ciphers for large amounts of implicit information which has been carefully condensed' (Botha, 2016: 17). 'Each of these techniques allows quicker access to the settings, narratives, backdrops, and characters Eminem is putting forward. We don't need (and don't have time) to gradually enter the text of a song like we might with a novel or a film: interaction must be instant, and all surplus material cut' (Fosbraey, 2022b: 28).

As well as the manipulations of content that are required to make songs an acceptable (or palatable) length for the average pop listener, songwriters are also working within a medium where a familiar structure is encouraged. In terms of the sound of a song, Levitin posits that 'too many chord changes, or unfamiliar structure, can lead many listeners straight to the nearest exit, or to the 'skip' button on their music players' (Levitin, 2008: 237), and Blume likens familiar structure as 'analogous to using proper grammar and punctuation to better communicate our ideas when we speak or write' (Blume, 2004: 3). This is why, as we see in the amusing (but suitably eye-opening) video '4 chords' by Australian comedy group Axis of Awesome, many of the most popular and enduring songs of the last sixty years have used the 'cliché' chord progression I-IV-V-vi (or inversions of it), including 'Don't Stop Believin'', 'You're Beautiful', 'Where Is the Love', 'Forever Young', 'Can You Feel the Love Tonight', 'Take Me Home, Country Roads', 'With or Without You', 'Let It Be', 'No Woman, No Cry', 'Down Under', '2 Become 1', 'Take On Me', 'When I Come Around', 'Africa', 'If I Were A Boy', 'One of Us', 'Poker Face' 'Paparazzi', 'Barbie Girl', 'Time to Say Goodbye', and 'Auld Lang Syne' (Axis of Awesome, 2011). In *Reading Eminem*, I also note that Eminem's three biggest selling songs on the UK charts, 'Lose Yourself' (vi-IV-V), 'Love the Way you Lie' (vi-IV-V-I), and 'Stan' (vi-IV-V-I) involve inversions of the sequence, with many more in his back catalogue including 'Like Toy Soldiers', 'In your head', 'Nowhere Fast', 'Hailie's Song', 'Mockingbird', and 'Headlights' (Fosbraey, 2022b: 4). As well as repeatedly using the same chord sequences, songwriters are also drawn towards tried and tested song structures, with the 'verse-chorus form' (Sloan and Harding, 2020: 47) estimated to be present in 'at least 95% of songs in the charts today' (Musical U, 2024). Both of these elements of the songwriting craft influence the lyrics, meaning, as Paul Weller says that 'sometimes you might have to go back and edit [...] words to make them fit rhythmically into a musical piece' (Rachel, 2013: 189). Jarvis Cocker tells us that although the protagonist in the song 'Common People' was based on a real woman, he added the fictional detail that she 'studied sculpture' because 'the line scanned better' (Dimery, 2013: 731), and Annie Lennox describes a rigorous editing process involving 'lots of overview and revisiting' to make her 'initial outpouring' of ideas fit into a song structure (Rachel, 2013: 321). When it comes to structure, though, the most widespread 'manipulation' is the use of rhyme, and, with their requirement for both vowel sounds and consonant sounds after them to be the same, 'Perfect rhymes' are the worst offenders, as they drastically limit the number of words a lyricist has to draw upon. So, unless they have been lucky enough for their initial idea to rhyme 'perfectly' throughout, any examples of such in the final lyrics will have involved a dilution, alteration, or shift in the original intention. Going back to Rita Ora, the song 'Shape of me', one of the tracks in her 'diary of the last few years' album *You and I*, includes these lyrics, written from the perspective of her mother:

> 'She said, "Don't you worry, babe, you got my blood in your veins"
> "I'll be here to catch you when your world is just about to break"
> She said, "Don't you worry, babe, you can't help the way you're shaped"
> "So you gotta go make peace with all the pieces that you hate"'
> (Ora, 2023)

Each of the end rhymes here are 'Assonance' rhymes (where the vowel sounds are the same, but the consonant sounds before and after them are different) instead of 'Perfect', but even though this makes more words available, it's highly unlikely that Ora's mother imparted her wisdom using an AAAA rhyme scheme. Which means Ora has altered what she actually said (if, indeed, she said it at all). And if she has chosen four of these words simply because they rhyme, we may be justified in questioning what other words exist because they scan well or fit a syllabic count.

If song structure can put limitations on the kinds of content an artist can produce (if they want to be commercially successful, anyway) genre conventions can be similarly inhibiting. For example, as a white rapper operating in a predominantly black genre, Eminem was initially positioned as an outsider in the hip-hop world, and it was important for him, especially early on in his career, to fit in with genre conventions. This included, but was not limited to, the profane language he used, which aligned itself with 'hip hop's street language' (Mesiti, 1993: 219) as well as the 'attendant violence, criminality, sexual "deviance," and misogyny' synonymous with the 'gangsta life' (Rose, 2008: 3). What is important to note with Eminem (and any artist for that matter) is that just because they are speaking about a lifestyle in their lyrics that is supposedly representing their true selves, it does not mean they're actually living it. As Westhoff notes, 'despite their long and documented histories of condoning lawlessness in various forms, rappers including Snoop, Ice Cube, Eminem, Jay-Z and many others are highly paid corporate spokesmen for mainstream brands' (Westhoff, 2017: 253).

Truth may also be manipulated because the artist wants to hold back or omit information they don't want to be public knowledge, or simply because it's just not that compelling. As The Streets' Mike Skinner says, 'the thing about the absolute truth is, it's not pretty, and not everyone is interested' (Skinner, 2012: 222). In the case of some songwriters, including Kurt Cobain, false biography can be invented to create more engagement with a song. Cobain presented the Nirvana song 'Something in the Way' as biographical, 'based around a story he used to tell about living under a bridge' (Cross, 2002: 57). This was later dismissed as a fallacy, an example of Cobain distorting his own biography to make for a good narrative (Cross, 2002: 57) with Cobain writing in his journal that he used 'bits and pieces of others' personalities to form [his] own' (Cobain, 2003: 95).

Other artists wish to present themselves in a way that makes them more relatable, regardless of whether it's an accurate representation of their lives or not. Paul Weller deems it 'important to be honest and reflect how you feel' but says it's 'also important to try and include the people that listen to your record, to make it open enough for them to go, 'Fuck me, I felt that as well;

I'm going through this [...]' (Rachel, 2013: 189), and although this can indeed lead to a deeper connection between artist and fanbase, it may work the other way if they sing about circumstances they simply can't relate to any longer, given their star status. Artists like Jennifer Lopez, Nicki Minaj, Drake, Jay Z, Kendrick Lamar, Eminem, and countless others get round this problem by looking to the past and speaking about times when they *did* face financial (or other) burdens, which both makes them relatable to a mass audience, but also subjects of admiration due to their self-made status and ability to triumph over adversity before arriving at their current fame and fortune (Fosbraey, 2022a: 75). Others, like Ella Eyre, stay in the present, as she does in the Sigala song 'Just Got Paid' where she sings: 'I know I drink too much, can't pay my rent this month/I should be saving up, but I just got paid/I'm broke [...]' (Sigala et al., 2018). By the time this song was released, though, Eyre had been credited as a co-writer on every track of her gold-certificated album *Feline* as well as multi-platinum-certified single 'Came here for Love', platinum-certified single 'Answerphone', and four other singles certified silver. Along with songwriting royalties, Eyre would also have earned recording artist royalties, and income from a 26-date tour to promote the *Feline* album (many of which were at O2 venues). Even working within an industry where artists can be 'screwed over' (Kelly, 2020), it's hard to imagine Eyre being 'broke' to the extent where she can't pay her rent, so this attempt at relatability risks looking like a 'rich person pretending to be poor', which can be 'obnoxious' and 'vile' (Lewis, 2013).

Sometimes untruths occur due to external factors. In 1999, for example, Eminem wasn't allowed to release the song 'My Name is' unless he changed the second clause in 'My English teacher wanted to fuck me in junior high, only problem was my English teacher was a guy' to '[...] thanks a lot, next semester I'll be 35' (Eminem & Jenkins, 2009: 48). Although the original lyric was likely as fictional as its replacement, the latter couldn't even be remotely truthful seeing as Mathers was only twenty-six when the song was released, making it impossible for him to be thirty-five 'next semester' under any circumstances. As this is clearly a lie, we must then question the validity of every other statement in the song, even though it wasn't what he *wanted* to say. This is also the case for the occasions where Mathers toys with critics in his songs, daring them to take his lyrics literally. About 'Who knew', he says:

> The whole idea behind this song was to try to make critics feel stupid. I think I countered everything that was said about me last year with The Marshall Mathers LP. Just like my next album will counter everything

the critics said this year [...] I just tried to make them look stupid and let them
know not to take every fucking thing I say literally.
—(Eminem, 2000: 100)

By speaking with his detractors head-on, Mathers is allowing his lyrical content to be influenced by external forces and shaping his language accordingly, inviting them to criticise him again in order to give him more ammunition for future releases. In such cases, we find him exaggerating even more than usual so as to be as inflammatory and controversial as possible and this leads to such utterances as 'Just bend over and take it like a slut, OK Ma?' (Eminem, 2000b), and, to guess what the press will write about him for writing such a thing, follows it up by speaking in their voice: 'Oh, now he's raping his own mother [...] and we gave him the Rolling Stone cover?' (2000b).

In many of Eminem's songs, it's quite straightforward to separate the fact from fiction, if only because Mathers would be serving numerous life sentences for the crimes he says he commits, but in other songs, it's harder for us to establish where the facts end and the fiction begins. One of the most prominent examples of this is 'Brain Damage', which sees Eminem flit between out-and-out fantasy and what seems like quite a believable biography-driven narrative about an incident at school where Eminem was 'harassed daily by this fat kid named DeAngelo Bailey' (Eminem, 1999). In this instance, not even Eminem's own explanation of events in his *The Way I am* book provides satisfactory closure regarding which parts of the lyrics were factual and which fictionalised, saying: '[...] some people think I'm making it up, but nope – that shit really happened. My brain really was fucking bleeding out my ear.' (Eminem & Jenkins, 2009: 78). The lyrics were deemed realistic enough for Bailey to sue Mathers, citing the lyrics as slanderous. Judge Deborah Servitto dismissed the $1 million lawsuit, and in her summing said that 'The lyrics are stories no one would take as fact/ they're an exaggeration of a childish act."' (Dansby, 2003). In describing lyrics as 'stories' and 'exaggerations', Servitto put forward a more accurate theory on lyrics than many critics have done over the years.

Sometimes, though, Mathers delights in playing with his audience to blur the lines between fact and fiction. He does this primarily through his lyrics, by alternately guessing what they think of him (see 'Hailey's Song'); directly questioning the power an artist is perceived to have over a listener (see 'Sing for the Moment'); and inviting criticism by flouting his position as a 'role model' and telling the listener to act in a certain, irresponsible way (see 'Role Model') (Fosbraey, 2015: 21), but also via his *annotations* on his lyrics via the 'Genius' website, a platform which 'celebrates [...] the lyrics, the stories behind the songs' (Genius, 2022), which is usually a space for fans to put forward their own interpretations about what songs 'mean'. On the site, Mathers writes a comment in response to the 'Shady XV' lyric: 'Pathological liar, oh, why am I such an asshole' (2014), saying '[…] or am I though?' (Genius, 2016a), and in a comment in response to 'Criminal' and the lyrics: 'The mother did drugs, hard liquor, cigarettes and speed' (Eminem, 2000f) he said: 'I meant that literally. My mom would LITERALLY grind up DVD's [sic] of the movie "Speed" & snort it' (Genius, 2016b).

It's also common for fan and critic theories on songs to become so widespread that they become accepted as fact. Since I've been aware of the song 'Teenage Kicks' by The Undertones, for example, I've heard it was 'about' masturbation (which has been denied by songwriter John O'Neill). I'd also believed critics' long-held assertions that Lou Reed's 'Perfect Day' was 'about' his 'battle with drug addiction' (Geoghegan, 2013), again, something that Reed himself denied, saying in a radio interview that the song was 'real simple. I meant just what I said' (Ingate, 2024).

When an artist is inevitably asked 'what's the meaning behind this song?' and they give a literal answer, it immediately closes down the different ways a listener can interpret it. A recent interview with Charli XCX about her song 'Apple', for example, saw her revealing its intended meaning when she said (look away now if you're not a fan of the gratuitous and erroneous use of the word 'like': like I've been like 'I want to write a song about my kinda sticky relationship with my mom and dad, which is 'Apple''' (Kimont, 2024). And once the writer's vague intention is revealed, the temptation is to elicit further meaning line by line, which leads to analyses such as: 'I wanna grow the apple, keep all the seeds' indicates a desire to nurture and preserve the positive aspects of her [XCX's] heritage' (Stay Free Radio, 2024). Contemporary artists don't even have to wait to be asked. In an Instagram post from earlier this month, Sam Fender announced the release of new song 'People Watching' with accompanying text saying it was 'about somebody that was like a surrogate mother to me and passed away last November' (Fender, 2024a). To those who didn't see the post, the opening lyrics 'I people-watch on the way back home/Envious of the glimmer of hope/Gives me a break from feeling alone' (Fender, 2024b) could hold any number of different meanings, but those who *did* are now limited to Fender's.

In *Reading Eminem*, I argue that the way we buy and digest music today can lead to us 'forming judgments based on the opinions of others before we've heard a note of the music' (Fosbraey, 2022b: 9), due firstly to the ease with which we can access reviews from fellow listeners (5,649 ratings and comments for Eminem's Revival album on Amazon, I note, and over 150 individual reviews via a google search), but also to websites' own 'product descriptions' or ratings. I do concede that there was a variation of this when hard copy music reigned supreme, with reviews in the music magazines and newspapers readily accessible, but such reviews were significantly fewer, and, one would hope 'all conducted having given the album a fair run and (hopefully) a considered and fair assessment' (Fosbraey, 2022b: 9). Some streaming sites also offer an overview of albums when listeners go to play them, with Apple Music offering this above the play button for Eminem's Revival: 'The divide between Eminem, lyrical savant and god of rap, and Slim Shady, a trigger-happy psychopath, has always been difficult to bridge. It's harder to hear shock-value sucker punches about domestic violence and disability—least of all because they risk discrediting the genuinely powerful moments that Eminem is so uniquely capable of' (Apple Music). Listening to the album after digesting this versus going to a shop, buying the hard copy, then going home to listen to the music without any other information will inevitably lead to two very different listening experiences. Sites like Genius Lyrics/Songfacts go even deeper, not just passing general opinion on albums and songs but offering insights into the 'meanings' of individual lyrics. Such sites may be throwbacks to a pre-1950s way of 'reading' texts, where 'critics were on the whole preoccupied with the question of how to determine a text's literary meaning as precisely as possible' (Freund, 1987: 69), but for a music fan researching a song online, it is likely they will very soon come across one of these sites. Whatever interpretation of the song they find on there, then, however misinformed or tenuous, it will become significant to them and influence their own opinion, whether consciously or unconsciously.

An article on the website Vulture entitled 'What is every song on Taylor Swift's *folklore* actually about?' identifies the problem with such a process (before moving on, without irony, to what the next song is 'about'), with its author saying 'my fear is this: remember when we found out "You Oughta Know" was about […] Joey from Full House? I'm worried we're going to find out "mad woman" is about, like […] Rainn Wilson. Praying it's not' (Gutowitz, 2020). Indeed: what happens if we find out that the songwriter's intention behind one of our favourite songs isn't as deep or meaningful as we'd hoped? That Paul McCartney's 'Martha My Dear' was an ode to his sheepdog, not a love interest, or that 'Total Eclipse of the Heart' was inspired by vampires (Pritchard, 2015)?

2.1.2. *Singer vs song*

David Byrne observes that 'even if I choose to sing someone else's song, it's assumed that the song was, when it was written, autobiographical for them, and I am both acknowledging that fact and at the same time implying that it's applicable to my own biography. Nonsense! (Byrne 2012: 155).

The fallout of the 'Blurred Lines' controversy, which saw an outpouring of criticism due to its 'trivialising sexual violence, objectifying women and "reinforcing rape myths"' (Wyatt, 2013) suggests that it can be the act of *singing* lyrics rather than writing them which makes us assume connection. The Pharrell Williams-produced 'Blurred Lines', credited to 'Robin Thicke featuring T.I and Pharrell', and written by the same (with Marvin Gaye later given a credit) was released in March 2013 and went on to hit number one in twenty-two countries (including the US) and achieve fifty-six platinum certifications. Since then, only two of Thicke's singles have charted in the US, at twenty-five and eighty-two (with the last coming in 2014), and his most recent album, released in 2021, stalled at number ninety-three in the Billboard Album charts. In other words, his recording career seems to have been irreversibly damaged by the controversy. Pharrell Williams, on the other hand, released single 'Happy' in November 2013 and saw it hit number one in thirty-three countries and go platinum sixty-seven times. And, although not reaching those heights again, Pharrell has continued to have success, with six gold and two silver certified singles under his own name, as well as fourteen platinums, five golds, and two silvers as a featured artist. T.I has similarly suffered no ill-effects to his commercial success, with each of his post-'Blurred Lines' albums reaching the US Billboard top twenty. It does seem, as critics Selden, Widdowson, and Brooker say, that we do assume that 'speech incarnates, so to speak, the speaker's soul' (Selden et al., 2005: 165), and that, as the 'speaker' on 'Blurred Lines', Robin Thicke is considered the only of the three writers who supported its inadvisable and uncomfortable lyrics.

2.1.3. The role of the listener

In his article 'Race [...] and Other Four Letter Words: Eminem and the Cultural Politics of Authenticity', Rodman asks why 'so many people find it so extraordinarily difficult to envision Eminem (and other rappers) as someone who might have enough creativity, intelligence, and artistry to fashion and perform a convincing fictional persona?' (Rodman, 2006: 105). As we've seen, the instinct of critic and fan alike is to go running toward the songwriter (or, indeed, singer) in search of answers, and although this often leads to responses like the one from Charli XCX, other writers offer no such definitive explanations. John Lennon was frustrated enough by critics attaching his lyrics to his personal life to write 'I am The Walrus' as a deliberate curveball and always avoided explaining the 'aboutness' of his songs, and Neil Finn said that he's always happy when people get things 'wrong' (meaning 'different' from his own intention) (Csathy, 2021).

Some lyricists don't even *have* a meaning in mind when they write. For the Weezer track 'Summer Elaine and Drunk Dori', Rivers Cuomo drew lyrics from 'a spreadsheet containing a couple of thousand random lines' (Song Exploder, 2016) to create a song which suggests a coherent, real-life event but where each line was actually 'from a completely different place, reassembled in an order that suggests a story that never happened' (Song Exploder, 2016). As well as potentially offering no definitive explanation, this searching for answers reduces a complex form that uses imagery, syntax, allegorical language, rhyme, perspective, and numerous rhetorical devices to create emotive, persuasive, and life-affirming, and life-changing content to nothing more than a puzzle than needs solving. In order to pay due attention to the settings, characters, language, and plots of songs, then, we need to stay 'inside' them, rather than looking towards the outside (which includes asking the artists what it means). The first step towards this is to avoid altogether the problematic waters of involving author, artist, critic, or anyone else to discern the meaning of a song and focus instead on our own interpretations. This aligns with Roland Barthes' 1968 essay 'The Death of the Author' (Barthes, 1977: 142) where he draws the power of interpretation away from the producer of the text and gives it to the receiver and, later, Collini, who observes that 'a text, once it is separated from its utterer (as well as its utterer's intention) and from the concrete circumstances of its utterance (and by consequence from its intended referent) floats (so to speak) in the vacuum of a [...] range of possible interpretations' (Collini, 1992: 41). Shifting the power balance over to the reader (or listener, in the case of song), requires us to respond to articles like '16 Songs That Don't Mean What You Think They Mean' (which provided us with the 'Total Eclipse of the Heart' is about vampires quote a few pages back) by saying 'actually, if I *think* they mean this, then they *do*', in the process changing the listening experience from a passive one into an active one, where we are involved in a collaboration 'akin to a performance' (McCaw, 2013: 71). When we think about it, reacting to a song and then forming our own interpretation, is a more natural process than heading straight for Google and searching for the artist's intention. Adrian Beard may have been referring to novels when he observes that 'when coming to a text "cold", without the benefit of extra information, it is likely that your first responses, your first ways into the text will [...draw] on your previous experience as a reader of texts' (Beard, 2001: 11), but we can expand this to song, too. Levitin says that 'as with other sorts of preferences, our musical preferences are also influenced by what we've experienced before, and [...] the types of sounds, rhythms, and musical textures we find pleasing are generally extensions of previous positive experiences we've had with music in our lives' (Levitin, 2008a: 242).

As our initial reaction to a song is coming from an intrinsic, unconscious place, then, it is not only a valid reading, but an essential one.

In his book *Reception Theory*, Holub notes that '[...] perhaps the most important activity readers undertake involves removing or filling out the indeterminacies, gaps, or schematized aspects in the text [...an activity known as concretization...] Since concretizations are considered the activity of individual readers, [however,] they can be subject to vast variation. Personal experience, moods, and a whole array of other contingencies can effect each concretization. Thus no two concretizations are ever precisely identical, even when they are the product of the same reader' (Holub, 1984: 25). This is certainly true in my case, where, for example, my 'readings' of Morrissey songs vary wildly from when I first listened as a 16-year-old, to where I am now, some 25 years later. My relationships, jobs, education, and exposure to art and media in those years has drastically impacted my view of the world, so it's natural that my reactions to certain lyrics have gone through a similar evolution. This plasticity of meaning partially fits with what Searle and Vanderveken call 'context of utterance', which involves 'the same sentence [...] uttered in different contexts to perform different illocutionary acts' (Searle and Vanderveken, 1985: 27) but, given that an 'illocutionary act' is defined by the *speaker's* intention, it doesn't quite fit. When discussing such flexibility of meaning in my classes, my favourite example to draw upon is the song 'Don't Dream it's Over'. Interviewed on Consequence's *The Story Behind the Song* podcast, its songwriter Neil Finn noted that people have generally interpreted the song title and refrain 'Don't Dream it's Over' in two different ways: the way he intended (and the way it's presented grammatically) as in 'it's not over, keep believing', but also taking it to mean 'don't bother hoping any more as it's pointless'. If we're just looking at the song title on Spotify, Youtube, the track-listing on a CD, etc., this second interpretation only makes sense if we add a comma to make it 'Don't Dream, it's Over', but if we're just *listening* to it, without seeing the title written down, it's easier to read it as such (although still a little bit of a stretch, perhaps, as there's no discernible paused between the words 'dream' and 'it's'). When (inevitably) asked what the meaning behind the song was, Finn initially demurred, speaking instead of how he enjoyed people taking different interpretations, noting that the same songs can be played at both weddings and funerals due to what they mean to the individual listener. In the end, he did answer, though, saying 'Don't Dream it's Over' was meant as a 'hopeful, positive statement [...] the first step to addressing things that are not right in your own personal life [...] I wasn't sitting there thinking people would use it as an affirmative anthem for years to come, but I've been delighted that it has been used in a variety of different contexts as an affirmation of hope'. We can see these 'different' contexts at work by examining four different performances of the song, and how each succeeds in determining its own meaning. First, we'll look at 1986s 'Don't Dream it's Over' music video, which, seeing as the song wasn't performed live until January 1987, means it's most people's first visual accompaniment. An 'Art' music video with a bit of 'Staged Performance' thrown in, the video 'has Finn walking through a house in which other members of Crowded House are sitting around, sometimes playing their instruments. It's a scene of nostalgic Australiana worthy of Men at Work. The house is a weatherboard [timber-clad exteriors typical to Australian homes]; we even see a slice of toast spread with Vegemite [...] When the organ solo comes, the windows of this house are suddenly arched and have stained glass. It's fitting in this hymn to home' (Ford & Heino, 2019). If we research a little more, we see that the video is actually Finn walking through his own life, starting with (as the intertitles at the bottom of the screen inform us) the present day at 'Osborne Street 1986' – Finn's current residence in Melbourne, and the year the song's release, then moving back in time to '78 Teasdale Street 1958 – Xmas' – Finn's childhood home in Te Awamutu, New Zealand and his first Christmas; '1965' – with no location information, we assume this is also Teasdale Street, where Finn would have turned 7 in the May; 'The Study – Te Awamutu' – presumably 1965 again – 'The Mission Room' (a room dedicated to worship) – again, presumably 1965; 'Dream Kitchen – 1966' – we're unsure if this refers to someone's 'ideal' kitchen, a place where dreams are conjured, or is a link to the song's title; then, finally, back to the present with the full band playing together in a garage or outbuilding. After playing a few bars of the song, Finn puts on an overcoat, says goodbye to the band, and exits into a wide, open field, which he walks across, away from the camera as the video fades out. Apart from Finn's movement through the various rooms and time periods serving as a visual representation of the lyrics 'travelling with me' and 'walking again', there's little else that works with the lyrics. What we do have is the feeling of nostalgia and a direct link to Finn's life, both of which invite us to interpret the song differently to how we might have without the visuals. As such, we may now be inclined to read the lyrics as Finn appreciating where he's come from and wanting to keep sight of his past, but acknowledging that we need to keep moving forward in order to achieve great things (like being in Crowded House). This is reinforced by Finn moving through the door towards the band at the lyrics 'get to know the feeling of liberation and release' (Crowded House, 1986) as he liberates himself from his past to grow and develop as a person. Each time the title and refrain 'Don't Dream it's Over' occurs, we are either moving into, or just arrived in a new room, suggesting that just because we've moved on, it doesn't mean that part of our lives is 'over'. The 'build a wall between us' (Crowded House, 1986) line, then, is a physical wall between rooms, but also a wall between us and our past, and the 'they' who are responsible for its existence, and also the 'them' from the line 'don't let them win' are the negative influences in Finn's life who are trying to separate the current him (popstar Finn) from his humble roots.

For our second performance of the song, we fast-forward ten years to 1996 and Crowded House's *Farewell to The World* concert, where on the forecourt of the Sydney Opera House, they played their final show before disbanding. Strangely (to me, at least), 'Don't Dream it's Over' had never been a regular set-closer for the band, but it was chosen to bring proceedings to a conclusion on this particular night, in the most emotional of circumstances. In the official recording, after finishing the song 'In Your Command' to rapturous applause and shots of a teary-eyed audience, Neil Finn says 'Thanks for having us, Sydney, and everywhere else that's watching, looking on. It's been a blast' (Knowles, 1996) as he looks across the stage at the rest of the band. The camera then switches from Finn to drummer Paul Hester, who, in tears himself, dabs at his eyes with a towel. We stay on Hester as we hear Finn play the opening chords of the song, which elicits the biggest cheer of the night. At the end, after an extended outro section where the crowd sings along with Finn to the chorus, the band-members embrace one another and, finally, take a collective bow. Finn looks jubilant, and, as it was his decision to dissolve the group (Mojo, 2024), that's understandable, but Hester looks devastated, and, looking back at the footage with the knowledge that he'd commit suicide in 2005 and therefore miss the band's later reunion (including a return performance at the same venue), it's an emotional watch. The 'Don't Dream, It's Over' reading we previously mentioned can actually be applied to him here, seeing as his dream of performing with the band has indeed come to an end, but, Hester aside, the title and refrain, performed in this scenario, says that fans shouldn't think that this is the end of the band, and this is backed up by the line 'you'll never see the end of the road while you're travelling with me' (Crowded House, 1986). Taking things a step further, with Finn now free to pursue a solo career, the line 'get to know the feeling of liberation and release' (Crowded House, 1986) now attached to this, and his celebration at the conclusion of the song.

Our third performance comes at The Royal Albert Hall in 1999 where Neil Finn played the song without Crowded House as part of the *Concert for Linda* – a benefit tribute to Linda McCartney who had succumbed to breast cancer the previous year. Sung in this setting, it's hard not to see the song now being directed at Paul, who shouldn't 'dream it's over', that is give up hope, or his life, or his love for Linda. We might also take the line 'there are battles ahead, many battles are lost but you'll never see the end of the road while you're travelling with me' (Crowded House, 1986) as Linda addressing Paul, who will inevitably face 'battles' as he deals with the grief of losing his wife of 2twenty-eight years, but ultimately he will be able to carry on because she will always be with him. In this instance, then, the central theme of the song is to stay strong and hold on to the hope of better times.

Finally, Neil Finn himself drops out as we look at Miley Cyrus and Ariana Grande's performance of the song at the *One Love Manchester* concert, held at Old Trafford Cricket Ground in 2017, a benefit for the victims of the terror attack at Grande's Manchester Arena show earlier that year. Grande and Cyrus had already made a cover version of the song in 2015 as part of *Happy Hippie Presents: Backyard Sessions* in support of The Happy Hippie Foundation, a non-profit organization set up by Cyrus in 2014, which 'supports homeless youth, LGBTQ youth and other vulnerable populations' (Happy Hippies, 2024), but although quite endearing, and significantly better vocally than the Old Trafford performance, it didn't carry anywhere near the same levels of emotion. And that's all down to the circumstances surrounding it, rather than the performance itself, which, if we're being generous, wasn't exactly either singer's finest moment, with it pitched several keys to low for Grande, and with Cyrus several hundred decibels too high in the mix. But quality scarcely mattered, and it certainly didn't impact the crowd's enjoyment, as people not even born when the song was written (and maybe not even when song was played at the *Farewell to the World* concert) sung along to the chorus, their faces filled with emotion. Initially, the lyrics' connection to tragedy at the Manchester arena appeared tenuous at best, and downright inappropriate at worst, with the line 'don't dream it's over' flirting with the uncomfortable suggestion that the attack wasn't an isolated incident and more would follow. Putting this aside for a moment, though, we see that the real connection comes with the lyrics 'they come to build a wall between us, we know they won't win' with it now becoming a statement of defiance against terrorism, declaring that, despite the terrorists' best efforts, the people of Manchester (and beyond) would stand united against anyone who tries to destroy their way of life. And, what's more, they will triumph. Revisiting 'don't dream it's over' with this in mind, we can now view it not as something inappropriate, but as another defiant statement against oppression which says that the people will keep on standing up against such violence and their resolve will never be beaten. In other words, don't dream that our freedom and way of life is over because of this tragedy. The central theme of the song in this context, then, is to stand united in the face of adversity.

Putting together the overall 'meanings' the lyrics take within these four performances shows us how flexible lyrical interpretation can be, with our central takeaways being:

1. Be true to yourself, don't lose sight of where you've come from, but keep evolving as a person.
2. Don't be too sad about Crowded House splitting up, as it might not be forever.
3. Paul McCartney should stay strong and keep his hope alive.
4. Stand united in the face of adversity.

One set of lyrics: four completely different interpretations based on when and where they were performed.

2.2. The Components of Lyrics

As Hopps goes on to say (albeit only in relation to the lyrics of Morrissey), 'if Morrissey is a "serious artist", and if a major element of that art is linguistic, we might reasonably expect his lyrics to repay this kind of attention' (Hopps, 2009: xii), and I agree that working in this spirit is both instructive and necessary if we are to see lyrics as a medium worthy of detailed textual analysis. It's telling that no 'literary criticism' has been developed with song lyrics in mind, so, I have made it a primary aim in my work to create a workable set of conventions, repurposing existing theory from the academic study of English Literature, including (but not limited to) New Criticism, Structuralism, and Close Reading. Importantly, though, to avoid the issues I mentioned with regard to Ricks and his resituating of song lyrics as poetry, I use these techniques in order to draw meaning from the lyrics as *songs*, meaning that it is necessary to reinterpret and rework the existing theory so that it applies to this format. In terms of Close Reading, McCaw's definition as 'the detailed and specific interpretation of a text through its language, considering the prevalent images, symbols, metaphors, and patterns it incorporates' (McCaw, 2008: 43) can be applied to song without any alterations, and I note in *Writing Song Lyrics* that we may benefit from such a technique when analysing songs with the kind of defined character, story, and structure we may find in prose or prose poetry. In *Writing Song Lyrics*, I focused on the Elvis Costello song 'Kinder Murder' as a case study for close reading analysis, using it as an example of what we may discover from a song using only what we find 'inside it'. This includes, I suggest, 'the title, the significance of the opening line, perspective, use of tenses, idioms, slang, ambiguity and confusion, characters, setting, and the relationship between the lyrics and the sound of the song' (Fosbraey & Melrose, 2019: 60–66).

A song like 'Kinder Murder' provides rich analytical possibility, and we can see that just from looking its title and opening line that we are presented with several possibilities and questions, designed to entice us as a listener, pique our interest, and draw us into the song. When analysing a title, Childs suggests we ask whether it 'is primarily denotative (as in descriptive) or connotative (that is, suggestive and allusive)' while also considering its 'range of meanings' (Childs, 2008: 107).

As I say in *Writing Song Lyrics*:

> The title of 'Kinder Murder' could be described as connotative because it offers a play on words, with these three possible, separate interpretations of the word 'kinder', none of which are definitive:
>
> 1. Kinder: showing the quality of benevolence. 'Kinder Murder' taken literally would suggest killing someone in order to be generous or merciful. The word kinder also suggests we need something to compare it to; it begs the question 'Kinder than what?' and needs us to fill in the blank in the sentence 'This murder is kinder than [...]' The phrase is a very odd juxtaposition between two dissimilar images.
>
> 2. Kinder: phonetically the same as kinda as in 'sort of' or 'type of' (this interpretation only really applies if we're just listening to the song without seeing its title or lyrical transcript, as it's [sic] clearly not written that way. This interpretation would suggest that the events in the song's narrative all amount to a 'kind of murder', perhaps referring to the characters themselves or the decline of society.
>
> 3. Kinder: German for 'children'. This interpretation, with the song title now being 'Children Murder', would fit the line 'The child went missing and the photo fit his face', but its pronunciation involves a different vowel sound on the 'i' sound to what Costello sings.

A title like this creates intrigue in a listener and gets us interested before we've [sic] even heard a single note' (Fosbraey & Melrose, 2019: 60–61) meaning that we have formed a relationship with the song (whatever that may be) in a similar way we might react to the title of a book or poem.

I then go on to explore the significance of the opening line, again using a quote from Childs to frame the discussion, where he states that the 'first line or sentence [...] serves as a prelude to the rest of the text' (Childs, 2008: 108) and suggests that we ask ourselves: 'Does it orient you by giving information? Does it throw you into the narrative as though you had entered a story in the middle?' (Childs, 2008: 108).

I write that:

> Our first line in 'Kinder Murder' is 'Here in the bar, the boys like to have fun'. The use of the word 'here' gives us a location to inhabit and places us directly in the action, allowing us to be there in the bar, watching 'the boys'. Depending on how we read the song, this opening line either starts the linear narrative of the story or serves as a present-day narrative from which we branch off into flashback, turning it into the final action in the song's timeline as it is the only event in the present, meaning it is the most recent. The use of the word 'bar' in the same sentence as boys means we can not apply the most common meaning ('young males') and must therefore look upon it as a group of young men. So, the title and the first line are very allusive and ask more questions than they answer (what is a 'kinder murder?'; 'where's the bar?' 'who are the boys?'), serving as 'lyrical hooks' for the listener and mirroring the opening of the first page of a novel, whose job it is to draw the reader in to the rest of the work
>
> —(Fosbraey & Melrose, 2019: 61–62)

In this way, Costello is using his craft to have as much impact as possible on the listener.

2.2.1. The art of persuasion

In his 2015 autobiography *Unfaithful Music and Disappearing Ink*, Elvis Costello asks the rhetorical question: 'can a mere song change people's minds? I doubt that it is so, but a song can infiltrate your heart and the heart may change your mind' (Costello, 2015: 393).

I write in my monograph *Viva Hate* that 'although originally envisioned by Aristotle to analyse political speech, rhetoric has been a key way of analysing the written word ever since and can be applied to any form of oration, be that via the spoken word, written word, or sung word. The rhetoric of song lyrics can therefore be analysed in the same way we might analyse a political speech, or a piece of print media' (Fosbraey, 2022a: 45). Leith notes that 'Rhetoric is, as simply defined as possible, the art of persuasion: the attempt by one human being to influence another in words' (Leith, 2012: 1), and as songs have been used to persuade the listener of various things over the years – not least persuading them to buy, download, or stream the track in the first place – they deserve to be analysed in this way, and in detail. My own work on the subject has examined the ways in which a variety of songwriters working in a variety of eras have used rhetoric as a way to express their viewpoints on a series of important and controversial topics from Billie Holiday's 1939 version of 'Strange Fruit' whose lyrics were 'designed to instil horror and disgust in the listener [...and urged] them to act' (Fosbraey & Melrose, 2019: 87) through to Eminem's 2020 track 'Darkness' which is a 'quest to prevent gun crime in America' (Fosbraey, 2022b: 38).

I write in *Viva Hate* that 'as a tool of communication, pop music is one of the best there is, and artists have been capitalising on it for decades (and will for decades to come, no doubt). This is something that 'rulers have understood throughout history and across cultures' (Dillane et al., 2018: ix), with music being used at political rallies, or election campaigns (see New Labour's 'Things Can Only Get Better'), and, of course, to protest.' (Fosbraey, 2022a: 47). Song also has the benefit of immediacy (or, at least, near-immediacy) in getting across its message, meaning it has the opportunity to respond to current affairs while they are still current, for example Neil Young's 'Ohio', a 'shocked response to the shooting of four student protestors at Kent State University' which was 'recorded and rush-released within a month' after the event (Inglis, 2003: 31, 92). Song also has the potential to reach enormous audiences with its messages, and in *Viva Hate*, I point to Taylor Swift's 2019 music video for 'You Need to Calm Down', a song which protested homophobia and sexism, and garnered tens of millions of hits in the days after its release (with the current number standing at over 308 million) as well as actively encouraging viewers to sign a change.org petition in support of The Equality Act. It is hard to imagine any other artistic format being able to create such action, and at such speed. In *Viva Hate*, I reflect on the importance of rhetoric when it comes to analysing song lyrics by dedicating forty pages to rhetorical analysis, beginning with an exploration of how songs in the Thatcher era of British politics persuaded us to dislike a person or group of people, and then moving on to 'hate in the golden age of hip-hop' where I discuss how groups like NWA and Public Enemy rallied against police brutality and racism and attempted to persuade the listeners of their viewpoints. As Horner and Swiss note, these two acts owed a lot of their success to this, as it 'resonated with people worldwide [...with] the music [becoming] a vehicle through which the oppressed recognize[d] each other and become more aware of their subordination' (Horner & Swiss, 1999: 61).

Let's examine the rhetorical techniques Plan B (the moniker for singer/songwriter/producer Ben Drew) utilises in the song 'ill MANORS' to, as Leith says, 'influence us with his words' (Leith, 2012: 1). For the most part, I'll try and stay 'inside' the song as much as possible in order to focus on the language, which will involve excluding its music video as well as the film *ill MANORS* and its accompanying soundtrack. But Kunow and Mussil assert that 'there is no interpretation without contextualisation' and that our understanding of any text 'depends on the historical, cultural, and social circumstances' (Kunow & Mussil (eds.), 2013: 1–2) that surround it, so we should at least spend a little time exploring both Drew's background, and the climate that led up to the release of 'ill MANORS' on 12 March, 2012 before delving into the song itself.

Born in 1983 in 'Forest Gate, East London' (Sawyer, 2011), 'one of two children in a single-parent family' (Green, 2010), Drew grew up against a backdrop of poverty, drugs, and violence (Palmer, 2012), which he later used as ammunition for lyrical content for his 'brutal, genre defying rap-poetry of debut album, [2006's] Who Needs Actions When You Got Words' (Little Bastard, 2012), which reached number thirty in the UK Charts. Follow-up album in 2010 *The Defamation of Strickland Banks* fared significantly better, hitting number one and going four times platinum, and by the time 'ill MANORS' was released, Drew had won three Ivor Novello awards (including best songwriter) and a Brit award.

In 2010 in the UK, after thirteen years of a Labour government, the General Election 'returned a hung Parliament' resulting in a 'Conservative-Liberal Democrat coalition' (UK Parliament, 2024) with the Conservative Party's David Cameron serving as Prime Minister, and the Liberal Democrats' Nick Clegg as his deputy. Prior to becoming Party Leader, Cameron had frequently stated that 'British society was broken and in need of repair' (Hayton, 2012: 136), and the notion of 'broken Britain' subsequently became a 'dominant theme of the pre-election campaigning' (Gentleman, 2010). Despite the Liberal Democrats' declaring an 'aspiration to phasing out tuition fees in their 2010 manifesto' (Butler, 2020), one of the coalition's first actions was to back a motion to almost treble the cap on University tuition fees from £3,290 to £9,000 a year (BBC News, 2010), something Labour leader Ed Milliband derided as 'cultural vandalism' which he predicted would 'set back the cause of social mobility by a generation and [...discourage] students from lower and middle-income families from going to university at all' (Helm & Asthana, 2010).

August 2011 saw 'the most severe civil unrest the UK had seen for a generation' where London was 'engulfed by 5 nights of fire and violence' before the 'uprising spread across England, including to the cities of Birmingham, Salford, Manchester, Liverpool and Nottingham' (Bell, 2021). Prime Minister David Cameron reacted by saying 'parts of our society are not broken but sick' (Aitkenhead, 2011).

When 'iLL Manors' was released, future Prime Minister Boris Johnson was halfway through his tenure as Mayor of London in 2012. Although stating that when he took on the role, London 'had four of the six poorest boroughs in the UK' but when he left 'had none of the bottom 20' (Walker, 2019), it was 'found that there were still four London boroughs in the top 10: Hackney, Barking and Dagenham, Tower Hamlets and Newham' (Walker, 2019), all of which are in East London.

The year 2012 also saw London hosting the Summer Olympics, with the Olympic Stadium (later renamed 'The London Stadium') and Olympic Village (later renamed 'East Village') both situated in East London. Despite global praise for the event (Lawrence, 2012), others were more critical, with Dr Penny Bernstock of University College London pointing to 'the homes that were demolished to make way for the Olympics in the first place' including 'Clays Lane [which] was the largest residential co-operative of its kind in the UK. Built in 1977, near where the Olympic velodrome now stands, it was an experiment in creating close-knit communities to help vulnerable single people in east London. Its demolition in 2007 eradicated 450 low-cost tenancies and left the community "shattered"' (Wainwright, 2022).

In a final bit of contextualisation before our analysis of 'iLL MANORS', it's worth noting what Owen Jones identified as 'Chav hate', which, he says, began to emerge as a force in mainstream culture in 2004' (Jones, 2012: 113) and, as the subtitle of his 2012 book *Chav* says, was an example of *The Demonization of the Working Class*. When I was growing up in East Kent in the late 80s/early 90s, the word 'chav' was regularly used as a term of endearment similar to 'mate' (apparently derived itself from the 'Romany word, "chavi" which means child' ((Bennett, 2012a) but it had now morphed into a derogatory term to describe 'a young person of a type characterised by brash and loutish behaviour and the wearing of designer-style clothes [...] usually with connotations of a low social status' (Bennett, 2012b: 146). Soon adopted by public and mainstream media alike, The Daily Mail soon ran a 'handy "A to Z" of chavs', which contained such charming observations as: 'A is for A-Level: something no Chav has ever possessed', and 'U is for Underage: What every Chavette is at the time of her first sexual experience' as well as jokes like: 'what do you say to a Chav when he's at work? Big Mac and fries, please, mate.' (Jones, 2012: 113–114). In recent years (thankfully) the derogatory use of the word has lessened, but it was most certainly still alive and well in 2011 when 'on Newsnight during the riots [...] historian David Starkey [...] attacked "chav" culture' (Vallely, 2012).

With our background work done, let's move on to our rhetorical analysis, starting with how Drew establishes a relationship with us.

McCloskey identify the six parts of a speech in classical rhetoric as 'The Exordium (an appeal to ethos, that is the character worthy of belief), the Narration (presenting the facts of the case), the Division (presenting what is to be proven), the Proof (the argument [...]), the Refutation (dealing with objection [...]), and the swelling crescendo of the Peroration' (McCloskey, 1994: xv).

We'll starting with 'The Exordium', which, when successfully employed, will 'put the audience into a receptive and attentive frame of mind' (Leith, 2012: 84). From a musical perspective, the song begins with violent, stabbing strings sampled from Peter Fox's 'Alles Neu', itself a sample of Shostakovich's 7th Symphony, which was 'written and first performed as German forces besieged Leningrad' and 'echoes with the pounding rhythms of war' (Service, 2016). This morphs into 'an explosion of drum'n'bass [...which] takes the song in a bloodier, more violent direction' (Cragg, 2012) and above it, Drew's vocal alternates between menace, sneering contempt, anger, and mockery. 'Political songs', Peddie says, 'are defined as such by virtue of their words, but many make their impact in tandem with their sonic elements, the emotionality of the music, the strength and confidence of the vocals' (Peddie, 2006: 4) and the sound of 'iLL MANORS' provides a suitably ominous and aggressive backdrop to Drew's words. Lyrically, the opening line of 'iLL MANORS' which, Blanton says should be 'impacting, concise, [...and] provocative]' (Blanton, 2010: 122) sees Drew saying 'Let's all go on an Urban Safari we might see some illegal migrants' (Plan B, 2012) and although he's using the first-person plural pronoun 'us' in the contraction 'let's', it's clear that he is employing 'verbal irony' to mimic the kind of people who would go on an 'Urban Safari', a term historically used to describe a type of 'slum tourism' where 'people of education' would 'turn themselves loose among the people [...in] the lowliest streets in the city' (Bender, 2011:138). This 'verbal irony', a technique which 'enables the speaker to convey his meaning with greater force by means of a contrast between his thought and his expression' (Dane, 2011: 126) is used by Drew throughout the song, allowing him to take on the voice of an authority, to 'attack a point of view or to expose folly, hypocrisy, or vanity' (Stringfellow, 1994: 3). As Bryant notes, though, 'because verbal irony involves attributed attitudes and beliefs of real or imagined persons [we...] must decouple these second-order representations, and infer the actual intentions' of the speaker (Bryant, 2011: 293). If we don't, and take all of Drew's utterances at face value, we see him embodying the kinds or opinions and terminologies he's seeking to rally against, which won't endear his to a listener who is sympathetic to working-class struggles. The listener is required to participate in the song, then, to recognise Drew's irony and separate his ironic statements from his literal. In asking this of his audience, Drew is treating them as equals who he refuses to talk down to by explaining his intentions. It may result in some people missing the point, but it's positioning him as the direct opposite of the patronising 'Urban Safarists' who have so dehumanised the working classes that they now view them as one might view animals on a savannah.

With this first usage of verbal irony, Drew is shining a light on how people who adopt such behaviours are ill-informed, out of touch, and pompous, and within a few seconds the line 'he's got a hoodie on give him a hug' (Plan B, 2012) tells us who these people are. Although David Cameron 'never actually said that anyone should "hug a hoodie"' (Birrell, 2012), the phrase was attributed to him by the Labour party due to a speech he made in 2006 where he called 'for more understanding of why young people commit crime' (BBC 2006). Suggesting that 'violence and hatred are not motive forces of their own' (Kruger, 2008) may have been a 'change from the froth and synthetic fury of Tony Blair' (Birrell, 2012), but, in reality, ended up presenting 'no new ways of thinking […] no new schemes, no new projects on the horizon that even [began…] to dent […the] problem of gang culture, feral youth, the Asbo generation' (Brown, 2011). And it's this which Drew takes issue with, positioning Cameron and his cabinet as the 'us' characters who pretend to understand working class issues but succeed only in remaining aloof and detached while failing to enact any positive change despite all their bluster. With the target of his ire now identified, Drew can turn his attention to aligning himself with the group he is targeting his rhetoric at. Borchers and Hundley say that 'persuasion is only complete when an audience member convinces himself or herself of what has been said by others' (Borchers and Hundley, 2018: 180), and in order for this to occur, they need to be able to identify with both the speaker and what the speaker is saying. This is achieved by the speaker (or 'rhetor') using 'one or more of three broad types of identification': finding common ground in terms of background; establishing an 'us-versus-them'; and showing that a community, group, or other collective is united in a common goal (using the word *we* in such a situation can be powerful in creating a sense of unity) (Borchers and Hundley, 2018: 180). Following on from his identification of the Conservative Government as his quarry, he further establishes the 'us-versus-them' idea by using the second person direct addresses 'you', 'your', 'yourself', 'you've', and 'you're' on twenty-seven separate occasions, with the word 'you', appearing nineteen times, the joint-most frequently used word in the entire song along with 'the'. With the 'them' in 'us-versus-them' firmly in place, Drew situates himself among the 'us' by using the first-person plural pronouns 'we' (including contractions 'we're', 'we've', and 'we'll') eighteen times, and 'us' three times – although, as we've seen, one of these was used to mimic the 'them'. And the identify of this 'us'? 'Chav', 'council estate kids'. As Hordsal suggests that audiences 'identify emotionally with narratives of personal experience' (Horsdal, 2012: 26), though, it's important that, as well as using first-person plural pronouns to situate himself as part of a group, Drew also uses first-person singular pronouns to show how he's personally involved, and he does so with 'I' (including the contraction 'I'll') appearing seven times and the first-person possessive pronoun 'my' thirteen times.

Another function of 'The Exordium' is an appeal to 'ethos', one of Aristotle's fundamental modes of persuasion which 'persuades through the representation of the speaker's character or judgement' (Lockwood, 1996: 67) and is reliant on 'personal credibility' (Shabo, 2010: 8). I say in *Viva Hate* that 'in order for artists to be able to persuade the listener of certain viewpoints or opinions, their authenticity needs to be unquestioned' (Fosbraey, 2022a: 68), and, considering the identity of the 'us', and 'the notion of "authenticity" […being] central to the working-class ethos, most particularly, moral authenticity' (Lott, 2013), it's particularly important to the success of 'ILL MANORS' that Drew is seen as 'authentic' throughout. In his article 'Authenticity as Authentication', Moore outlines the different types of authenticity, saying: First-person authenticity 'arises when an originator (composer, performer) succeeds in conveying the impression that his/ her utterance is one of integrity […] [Second-person authenticity] occurs when a performance succeeds in conveying the impression to a listener that the listener's experience of life is being validated, that the music is "telling it like it is" for them […] [Third-person authenticity] arises when a performer succeeds in conveying the impression of accurately representing the ideas of another' (Moore, 2002: 214). Drew employs 'first-person authenticity' and 'second-person authenticity' throughout the song. The former occurs via his knowledge of the East-End area, the language that he uses, and, perhaps, most importantly, his accent, which provides 'localness', 'independence', and 'authenticity' in what is, essentially, a 'highly performed […] constructed' medium (Montgomery & Moore, 2017: 218), and the latter through his awareness of what it's like to grow up in areas where residents are seen as 'scum' by the media ('council estate kids, scum of the earth), patronised by the government ('let's all go on an Urban Safari'), and endlessly stereotyped as violent ('that means council-housed and violent), drug-taking ('every single one of us buns the herb'), benefit-scroungers ('give us free money and we don't pay any tax') (Plan B, 2012).

The aforementioned verbal irony is also an appeal to ethos, as, according to Weigand, 'irony helps to debunk the private images and ideals that have been imprinted on one's mind by external authorities […and] the ironic rebellion against external authority is meant to prove that the individual is not passive but rather self-determining and thus free' (Weigand, 2008: 177). Presenting himself in this way, as a rebel who is standing up for what he believes in, even if it means actively railing against an authority (and hang the consequences), Drew is cementing his personal credibility and moral authenticity, and making his audience believe that his is a character worth getting behind.

The second of the 'six parts of speech' is Narration, where the speaker is supposed to present the facts of the case. Linking with another of Aristotle's fundamental modes of persuasion, 'logos', which uses 'rational analysis [...combined with] persuasive language' (Shabo, 2010: 8), this is Drew's opportunity to show how well-informed he is, and how well he can articulate his points. Undoubtedly one of Drew's strengths in 'iLL MANORS' is how intelligent he comes across, showing knowledge about government policy, healthcare, environmental issues, social economics, and community engagement, while also engaging with several examples of clever wordplay, which, through their subtext, he is able to add additional information and opinion. In the line 'just another brick in the wall', for example, he is using a double meaning, first to demonstrate how, in schools, pupils from these communities are merely considered faceless entities without individuality, and second, by drawing upon the lyric 'we don't need no education' from the Pink Floyd song 'Another Brick in The Wall Part 2' further mocking the establishment's stereotypical view that working class people are both unintelligent (gleaned from the grammatically correct 'we don't need no') and undesiring of education.

The 'Division' part of speech, also known as 'the case [...] sets forth the points agreed on by both parties and the points to be contested' (Aune, 2003: 63) and is the speaker's opportunity to show their awareness of both sides of an argument before moving onto the 'proof', where they will persuade the audience that their side is the correct one. What both the 'us' and 'them' characters in the song agree on is that there are social and economic disparities in Britain that are driven by a class divide, and that there needs to be systemic change. Demonstrating each side's approach to these issues, Drew, through mimicry, shows the Conservative Party's solution to broaching these divides is to immerse themselves in the working-class culture by observing them in their natural habitat (via their 'Urban Safari'). Drew also tells us how they are 'eco-friendly', sympathetic to the housing needs of the working classes and managed to build 'an entire Olympic village [...] without pulling down any flats' (Plan B, 2012). On the side of the 'us' group, Drew shows us that the points to be contested are the Government's belief that they 'think [...they] know how life on a council estate is' (Plan B, 2012) based on what they've 'read or heard', when they are actually just swallowing a set of stereotypes perpetuated by the media (which may or not be the same media who came up with the 'A to Z of Chavs'). They are also out of touch 'rich kids' who fail to listen to the voices of the working classes and continue marginalising them.

Although the English word proof suggests 'logical rigor or access to concrete evidence' (Gunderson, 2009: 292) the 'proof' part of rhetorical speech instead requires 'confirmation and refutation so as to effect persuasion' (Gunderson,

2009: 292), which means that the 'proof' and 'refutation' of speech are essentially two sides of the same coin, with one side asking the speaker to persuade us why they're right, and the other side asking them to persuade us why their opposition is wrong.

In 'iLL MANORS', Drew deals almost exclusively with the side of refutation. First, he tells us that the Government's 'Urban Safari' was a failure because they ended up perpetuating stereotypes by using the word 'chav' and worrying they'd get 'mugged' if they showed compassion. Next he says that the Government's 'eco-friendliness' and 'Olympic Village' build, which were painted as a positive, are actually examples of more verbal irony, where Drew is saying that the Government's promises of 'protecting our environment' (GOV.UK, 2015a) and providing 'opportunities for communities to shape the design of their areas' (GOV.UK, 2015b) were just the 'smoke and mirrors' of politics (Plan B, 2012), and that the destruction of the Clays Lane estate is evidence that they would ignore such things if they stood in the way of economic growth. Finally, as well as providing more wordplay, the lines 'there's no such thing as broken Britain, we're just bloody broke in Britain, what needs fixing is the system (Plan B, 2012) shows Drew to be informed about the Conservative Party's 'pre-election campaigning [where...] the notion of broken Britian [...was] a dominant theme' (Gentleman, 2010), as well as hitting back at it by saying that if it is indeed 'broken', it's because of poverty, and the system's failure to address it. By attacking the government in this way, Drew is engaging in what Culpeper defines as 'communicative aggression', which involves 'any recurring set of messages that function to impair a person's enduring preferred self image' (Culpeper, 2011: 20) and 'social harm' which is defined as 'damage to the social identity of target persons and a lowering of their power of status [and] may be imposed by insults, reproaches, sarcasm, and various types of impolite behaviour' (Culpeper, 2011: 20).

Where song really differs from speech (and, indeed, other forms of entertainment), is its use of repetition. The repeating of certain words or lines is a standard rhetorical technique, of course, and 'can acclimate readers to ideas, offering repeated opportunities to make sense or to come to a gradual understanding' (Kirsch, 2014: 67), but in song, we see entire passages of text repeated several times over due to the use of choruses. Choruses, Johnson observes in his book *Pop Music Theory* contain 'the message of the song, or the main point the lyricist is trying to convey' (Johnson, 2009: 26), and in doing this may spread the peroration throughout a song instead of leaving it to the end, like most classical speech. In 'iLL MANORS', the chorus appears on three occasions and is also the last thing we hear before the backing track gives way to the 'Alles Nou' strings we heard at the beginning (which 'bookending' the song as it does, suggests we're stuck in a perpetual loop), so is clearly very important to whatever message Drew is trying to convey, and what he is trying to persuade us to think. The chorus may be the peroration, then, but it may just as conceivably come via the final verse, where Drew's voice is heightened in the mix against a scaled-down backing and he delivers his lyrics with a causticity that lends real menace to every word. This verse also drops the verbal irony that has been used throughout the song, and for the first time Drew speaks directly to the 'politicians', while also telling us, with the line 'you bloody rich kids never listen' (Plan B, 2012), that the 'rich boy' he'd been referring to in the choruses was also a politician, and likely one of those who'd come to Drew's 'Manor' on the 'Urban Safari'. It also ties together other things he'd been referring to in the song so far, simplifying the message in order to create a tight conclusion that couldn't be misread due to its subtlety, satire, or irony. Here, Drew says that the politicians have come up with initiatives to mend 'broken Britain' without listening to (or understanding) the people whose lives will be impacted by them, and if there isn't a change in the system, there will be continued uprisings from the working-classes. Leith's definition of peroration as 'the section which is supposed to sum up the argument and 'move the audience to tears of pity or howls of rage' (Leith, 2012: 104) certainly fits with this final verse.

Drew also (whether intentionally or unintentionally) utilises what journalists refer to as 'the 5 W's and 1 H' which involves the body of a news story, article, or feature containing information on 'who, what, when, where, why, and how [...] to hold the reader's interest' (Vos, 2018: 221). Drew uses the words 'who', 'where', and 'when' on two occasions each, 'what' ten times, and 'how' once, to tell us 'who' he's talking about; 'where' the events he's describing are taking place; 'when' they are occurring; 'what' their impact is; and 'how' 'life on a council estate is' (Plan B, 2012). The only 'W' that's missing is 'why', but encouraging the listener to ask that themselves (i.e. why do such behaviours exist?) is one of the rhetorical successes of the song.

2.3. Storytelling

With my analysis of Eminem's songs in *Reading Eminem*, I acknowledge the importance of storytelling to his output by dedicating an entire section to it, applying the 'theories of narrative' Negus says are often overlooked in the analysis of popular songs and exploring the different ways he uses narrative. I begin the 'Eminem and Story' section by looking at how song lyrics differ from other media when it comes to narrative and story (other than the obvious, musical elements).

In his paper 'Narrative, Interpretation, and the Popular Song' Keith Negus observes that 'the popular song – one of the most pervasive narrative forms that people encounter in their daily lives – has been almost entirely ignored in the vast literature on narrative [...with] theories of narrative [...] rarely been foregrounded in the study of popular songs' (Negus, 2012: 368). Concerning hip-hop, Edwards says that 'most stories in [...the genre] follow a pattern similar to traditional stories in books, movies, and TV series [...with] characters, settings, and a structured plot – a beginning, a middle, and an end' (Edwards, 2009: 35), and this is particularly evident in Eminem's body of work, where he employs a variety of different characters, settings, and narrative scenarios. Eminem even draws upon the epistolary format in the song 'Stan' which 'stretches the narrative possibilities of rap' (Taylor, 2019) via a series of letters and recordings from the titular character, then creates a sequel for it 13 years later via 'Bad Guy', described by Spin Magazine as 'a seven-minute Charlie Kaufman movie' (Weingarten, 2013). Both of these songs also embellish the narrative by adding a series of sound effects (like the sounds of thunder, scratching pencils, screeching tyres, tape being unravelled), techniques used frequently in radio to set the scene and describe something succinctly and quickly, 'using airtime economically because it can release precious seconds for something else' (Starkey, 2004: 192).

Allen observes that 'meaning becomes something which exists between a text and all the other texts to which it refers and relates, moving out from the independent text into a network of textual relations' (Allen, 2000: 1), and although this was written in reference to Intertextuality in literature, it is a useful way of highlighting how Eminem links different narratives together to form a larger story. One of the ways in which he does this is via the album format, and although in his 2015 book *Rap and Hip Hop Culture*, Fernando Orejuela says that modern music fans 'question the rationale behind purchasing an entire album as opposed to just a couple of singles that are standouts or hits', to reject the format means they miss 'the holistic intention of the artist, the comprehensive story of a particular time and place [...] It's as if we crop the singular image of the creation of Adam to represent the whole narrative of Michelangelo's Sistine Chapel fresco panels: iconic representation, perhaps, but not enough' (Orejuela, 2015: xii). This is, perhaps, most relevant when considering the concept album, and although Eminem has never made an album which would technically be classified as one, his 2009 release *Relapse* is at least conceptual in that it deals with the theme of addiction throughout. As such, I analyse the album as a single entity, looking at the songs as if they were scenes in a film fitting together to form an overarching narrative. And it *does* work as a single story, even if that story is an 'antiplot' narrative which 'skips helter-skelter through time or so blurs temporal continuity that an audience cannot sort out what happens before and after what is told in nonlinear time,' (McKee, 1999: 45) and uses Inconsistent Realities which 'mix modes of interaction so that the story's episodes jump inconsistently from one "reality" to another to create a sense of absurdity' (McKee, 1999: 54). But this technique fits well with the subject matter and mirrors Eminem's mental state in the lyrics as he lurches from one bizarre drug-fuelled scenario to another.

I also observe that Eminem uses skits to weave together continued narrative threads, in particular the ones involving the fictionalised versions of Steve Berman (real-life CEO of Interscope records) and Mathers himself, which run from 1999s *The Slim Shady LP* all the way to 2018s *Kamikaze*, skipping *Recovery* and *Revival* along the way' (Fosbraey, 2022b: 30). Producer Prince Paul observes that one of the benefits of skits are to give the listener 'more of a sense of [...the artist's] personality and feel a little closer to them' (Rubin & Aaron, 1999: 95), and Eminem tends to use the majority of his skits in this way, 'allowing the listener the experience of almost eavesdropping in on various episodes and getting fly on the wall/behind the scenes access to his life' (Fosbraey, 2022b: 30). I note that Eminem's skits also often function as comic interludes, frequently sandwiched between two tracks with dark and/or violent content, and can be analysed as individual tracks in isolation as we would any other song. I examine 'Steve Berman' on *The Eminem Show*, which 'even as a 33 second audio clip, [...] carries with it a complete narrative [...and what] Booker would define as an 'Overcoming the Monster' story (Booker, 2004: 21–29), with Eminem cast in the role of underdog hero to Berman's Corporate Monster' (Fosbraey, 2022b: 36). The skit also satisfies what McKee defines as a 'Classical Design' structure (McKee, 1999: 45), with 'Causality' arising from Berman's words leading Eminem to shoot him; a 'Closed Ending' with Berman shot and presumably dying; told in 'Linear Time' (the 33 second episode moves linearly from beginning to end without any jumps); with an 'External Conflict' (Eminem vs. Berman); 'Single Protagonist' (Eminem); 'Consistent Reality' (it all happens in the reality of the story); and an 'Active Protagonist' (Eminem)' (Fosbraey, 2022b: 36).

Finally, I take Allen's 'textual relations' theory as far as possible, to put forward a theory that we are able to view Eminem's entire career lyrical output in terms of one single narrative, 'ranging from him being a couple of months old in 'Cleanin' out my Closet' to him in the present day via *Music to be Murdered by Side* B, [...where he details] how he's dealing with Covid 19'. (Fosbraey, 2022b: 31). In order to analyse how the different events in his lyrical output form a linear storyline, I draw upon a classic three act structure of story, as defined by Yorke (2014) to demonstrate a visible shift from Inciting

Incident (which I suggest is Mathers wanting to escape poverty and provide a better life for his daughter), through to Resolution (where Eminem overcomes the addiction he faced during the Crisis phase of the story but remains an addict in recovery).

As well as Eminem deploying definable narrative structures, he also uses a number of narrative techniques in his lyrics, including what McQuillan identifies as 'dialogic narrative: a polyphonic narrative composed of the interaction of several voices none of which is superior to, or privileged above, any other (in the song 'Guilty Conscience'); hypodiegetic narrative: a narrative embedded within another narrative (in the song 'Bad Guy'), and satellite: A minor plot event not logically essential to the narrative action' (in the D12 song 'My Band') (McQuillan, 2000: 315-328). Eminem also uses the choruses in his songs as a way to bring in different voices and perspectives from guest artists in *dialogic* narratives where 'the voice of the narrator [Eminem's] is not taken as the single point of authority in the narrative but as one contribution to knowledge among others' (McQuillan, 2000: 317). In songs like 'Love the Way You Lie', for example, the guest artist's voice (Rihanna's in this case) offers up their own opinion within the narrative and functions independently as a genuinely different perspective to the events Eminem details through his narration. In most choruses, however, Eminem inhabits the voices of his guest artists, getting them to speak *for* him. I observe that, in 'an inaccurate review of the song 'Headlights', Johnson of the *NME* says that 'In the final verse, he [Eminem] discusses mortality, saying that should the plane crash he was OK. "I am not afraid to die," he raps' (Johnson, 2013). Eminem does not rap this, Nate Reuss sings it, but, unintentionally, the reviewer does get to the nub of the matter, for even though the words are not coming out of his mouth, this *is* still Eminem's voice: he is just using Reuss to say the words for him. We can see the set-up for this in the final verse, where Eminem raps 'I wrote this on the jet', and in the final chorus, Nate Reuss sings 'If the plane goes down' (Fosbraey, 2022b: 48).

In terms of what lyrics can achieve in terms of narrative, they have a great deal in common with short story or short film. Unlike the novel or feature film, a short story or short film doesn't have the time to slowly develop characters and allow us to bond with them over time, and there's no space to slow-burn narrative progressions, either. The same is true for lyrics, but that doesn't mean songs can't have character or narrative arcs or even follow classic three or five act structures. Parker states that a three act structure should do the following: 'Act 1: Establish; Act 2: Develop; Act 3: Conclude. At the beginning of any narrative you have to establish the parameters of the narrative in the audience's mind [...] answering a number of simple questions like "where are we?" to "what is this about?" [...] the second act [...] is the developmental part of the narrative [...] the third act is where you draw the narrative to its conclusion and provide a sense of closure' (Parker, 1999: 27–28).

If we look at Eminem's 'Stan' as an example, we can see this technique applied quite clearly: Act 1 involves verse 1, where Stan is introduced as a character, and the plot is introduced (Stan wants to hear back from Eminem, his idol); Act 2 involves verses 2 and 3, where we have a development of Stan's character, including more information on his fragile mental state and his relationship, and an escalation of his rage at Eminem not replying to his letters; Act 3 rounds off the story as Eminem responds to Stan's letters before realising it was his murder/suicide he'd heard about on the news (the song ending with this realisation: '[...] Come to think about it, his name was—it was you, damn [...]' (Eminem, 2000c). The choruses in this instance, sampled from Dido's 'Thank You', serve as a satellite narrative or subplot where Stan's girlfriend mournfully reflects on the misery Stan is causing her. This idea is reinforced by the music video where Dido plays the girlfriend, bringing her originally disconnected narrative inside the overall storyline.

As we will see shortly, staying 'inside' a song only gives us a partial picture of the overall whole, and to analyse the text fully, we do need to step outside at some point. But spending this time focusing on specific literary and narrative devices is essential if our desire is to conduct a proper, in-depth analysis that affords the song the close attention it requires (and deserves).

Chapter 3

GOING OUTSIDE

So far we have discussed the benefits of focussing our attentions only on what is contained within the text, and while such analysis is vital to my suggested way of reading popular song, there is also much to be gained from continuing our research to some elements beyond this. Indeed, some songs, which perhaps are not as narrative or language-driven, require such an approach in order to show us anything meaningful. This section will discuss how my work has looked at what songs can offer us in terms of cultural significance, the difference between real events and their lyrical representations, how the format we listen to music in influences our readings, and to what extent visual materials impact upon our relationships with songs.

3.1. The role of the Artist

3.1.1. Cultural significance

With regard to Nicki Minaj's 2013 song 'Anaconda', I write in *Writing Song Lyrics* that 'more significance comes when we begin to look outside the lyrics and consider their place in the wider world of pop music' (Fosbraey & Melrose, 2019: 68). Stephen Greenblatt (1995: 226) suggests a series of questions be asked in order to look at the types of cultural commentary present in texts, and with my suggestion that *song* be considered as a text, provides a useful exercise in demonstrating how 'Anaconda' benefits from applying such cultural analysis. Greenblatt asks us to consider:

1. What kinds of behaviour, what models of practice […] this work seem to enforce
2. Why might readers at a particular time and place find this work compelling
3. [Whether there are…] differences between my values and the values implicit in the work I am reading
4. Upon what social understandings […] the work depend[s]

5. Whose freedom of thought or movement might be constrained implicitly or explicitly by this work
6. What [...] the larger social structures with which these particular acts of praise or blame [...] might be connected?

(Greenblatt, 1995: 226)

Staying 'inside' the song when answering these questions functions only in offering 'a fairly basic first-person narrative from a narrator [...] who speaks about past relationships, drug taking, money, and violence' (Fosbraey & Melrose, 2019: 66), but when moving outside, we are presented with important information that would not be accessible were we to stay inside. We are able to, for example, observe that large sections of the song are sampled from Sir Mix-a-lot's 'Baby Got Back', discuss the subsequent implications of a female artist using such samples, or 'consider the video's impact on the lyrics – a video which is, arguably, more famous/infamous than the song itself.' (Fosbraey & Melrose, 2019: 68). The sample and the video allow us to form an analysis that the song functions as a feminist statement about the historic objectification (and vilification) of black women's body shapes and that the female body can be used as its owner sees fit, without the validation of the male gaze, a reading that certainly is not possible when considering just the music and lyrics of the song. Moving outside the song in this way opens up the discussion (and, indeed, analysis) to these wider themes, and I expand upon this in my chapter 'Girl Power?' in *Viva Hate* where I suggest that our appearance-obsessed culture extends to music. This results in a situation where, as McCallum and Dzidic suggest '[...] an artist's image and body seem to be more important commodities than the music they write and perform' (McCallum and Dzidic, 2019: 405). Pointing to Andrea Dworkin's 1974 quote that: 'In our culture, not one part of a woman's body is left untouched, unaltered [...] from head to toe, every feature of a woman's face, every section of her body is subject to modification, alteration' (Dworkin, 1974: 112). I observe that nearly fifty years later, things have only become more extreme, with Nicki Minaj herself feeling the need to undergo body augmentation surgery due to feeling 'insecure' because of comments made by label boss Lil Wayne. (Sanders, 2022). I note that this then has a knock-on effect upon women in general via the following cycle:

1. Minaj is coerced into getting body augmentation by a man.
2. In turn, she feeds this male idea of 'ideal' body shape into her lyrics, e.g. in ASAP Ferg's 'Plain Jane (remix)' where she raps: 'My body shaped like Jeannie, booty dreamy, waist is teeny', or in 'I'm Out', 'Flawless', 'Anaconda', 'Throw some mo', 'Fefe', or 'Monster' where

she similarly describes her big bum, small waist and large boobs body type, going as far as rubbishing other women who haven't got the same.
3. This then influences other women, with Bursztynsky noting in 2019 that: 'buttocks augmentations [...] have more than doubled since [2013]' (Bursztynsky, 2019)

(Fosbraey, 2022a: 14–15)

In order to address Greenblatt's assertion that we need to consider what social understandings the work depend upon it is important to examine the genre Minaj is working in, and its history of behavioural expectations. I note in *Writing Song Lyrics* that 'such is the importance attached to the music video of 'Anaconda' that it is almost impossible to find any kind of review/analysis of the song that ignores it' (Fosbraey and Melrose, 2019: 68), but the video, functioning as what Railton and Watson define as an 'Art Music Video' which 'operates as a site of creative expression which variously works as an aesthetic complement to the song or vies with it for artistic consideration' (Railton and Watson, 2011: 51–52) does distract us from the fact that Minaj's lyrics align themselves with the subgenre 'gangsta rap', focusing as they do on 'the violence, criminality, sexual deviance, and misogyny synonymous with the "gangsta life"' (Rose, 2008: 3). So, despite the fact that 'Anaconda' succeeds in 'co-opting a canonized [sic] hip-hop tune concerning the triumph of the male gaze and inverting it into a declaration of femme supremacy' (Time Out editors and Amy Plitt, 2018), it is also working within the limitations of subject matter the genre conventions allow.

I conclude my chapter 'Featuring [...] Nicki Minaj' by saying that much of Minaj's own work 'appears to endorse misogynistic, objectifying, and often violent utterances' (Fosbraey, 2021: 49–50) but the hip-hop genre itself is saturated with these themes (Oware, 2018: 3) so, the simple fact that she is working within a genre that is so male-dominated is testament to her strength and importance as female artist, adding a level of complexity that goes far beyond lyrical content. Leith notes that 'Rap is [...] a constant discussion of what the rapper is about to do, his credentials for doing it, "shout-outs" to the crew with whom he intends to do it and "disses" to members of enemy crews who propose trying to prevent him' (Leith, 2012: 86), and this raises two points: 1. The use of male pronouns shows that even critics are helpless to see hip-hop as anything other than male-owned, and 2. If women are to gatecrash this world, they need to act in the same way as the men who occupy it in order to appear 'authentic', something Armstrong identifies as being 'essential for an artist working in the hip-hop genre (Armstrong, 2004: 336). As I note in *Reading Eminem*, 'a bona-fide "authentic" hip-hop artist will

[also] be self-made and will have been through a number of hardships before arriving at fame and fortune' (Fosbraey, 2022b: 123), and Minaj was quick to establish this soon after arriving on the mainstream scene, detailing her 'poor childhood' in an interview with NME in 2012 (*NME*, 2012).

3.1.2. Making it personal

In his book *Playing To The Crowd*, Baym comments that fans' 'criticism of the music is one thing, but the unbound participation that social media afford [sic] leads to far more criticism of the musicians themselves [...where people are] happy to blur the boundaries between you and your music, or between you as a person and you as a persona' (Baym, 2018: 167). There are hundreds of examples of such behaviours, but one of the most oft debated in recent years has been the case of Morrissey, where 'on various social media platforms, users have repeatedly classified the former Smiths frontman as 'cancelled' for his views' (Johnson, 2019) which have been 'widely criticised and ridiculed, with many accusing [...him] of racism' (Grieg, 2018). Jonze notes that it 'can be difficult – painful, even – to untangle the things you love about him from those you despise' (Jonze, 2019), and it's hard to find an artist who, throughout their career, has so dramatically split opinion. On one side we have a devout fanbase, a 'dedicated legion of followers who treat each Morrissey show as a quasi-religious experience' (Jacobson, 2017: 5) who ensure that every one of his albums reaches the top 10 of the UK album charts, and on the other, numerous social media groups exist with titles such as 'Morrissey hate club', 'Morrissey hate page', and 'Fuck Morrissey, I hate him' (Fosbraey, 2022a: 102–103). As evidenced by the t-shirts bearing the slogan 'Love The Smiths, hate Morrissey' that can be found online, a number of Morrissey's biggest critics seem able to draw a neat line between The Smiths and Morrissey's solo output by separating Morrissey from the band, and Morrisey himself has declared 'an obvious media shift to delete me from being the central essence of The Smiths' (Skinner, 2024). As Morrissey says, though 'this cannot work because I invented the group name, the song-titles, the album titles, the artwork, the vocal melodies, and all of the lyrical sentiments came from my heart' (Skinner, 2024). In his chapter 'Fanatics, Apostles and NMEs', Snowsell 'examines the difficulty many fans of Morrissey find themselves in when the subject of their admiration engages in the mediated public sphere by uttering statements and adopting positions which seem to conflict ethically and philosophically with the more liberal and progressive views commonly attributed to The Smiths' (Snowsell, 2011: 75). If The Smiths' views could be considered progressive, then the same must also be afforded to Morrissey's solo output, rallying as it does against racial and

LGBTQ+ inequalities ('America Is Not The World'), toxic masculinity ('I'm Not A Man'), trophy hunting ('I Am Not A Dog On A Chain'), whaling ('I Wish You Lonely'), disablism ('November Spawned a Monster'), bullfighting ('The Bullfighter Dies'), and class snobbery ('Teenage Dad on His Estate'). There are also, however, the songs 'Bengali in Platforms' and 'The National Front Disco', which have each been criticised, the former for being 'possibly well-meaning but deeply patronising and utterly out of touch with the sensibilities of [Morrissey's] very hip Asian fans' (Stubbs, 2019) and the latter as engaging with 'far right and fascist imagery' (Jonze, 2019). Both claims have been counter-argued by other critics (and Morrissey himself), but even if these songs weren't intended to be inflammatory or offensive, what can't be ignored is that Morrissey has used language that could be deemed such, which despite his steadfast defence of his right to free speech, could at the very least be considered misguided or naïve. Horner and Swiss suggest that lyrics 'help determine how artists are perceived by audiences, what they seem to "stand for"' (Horner and Swiss, 1999: 87), but if the anti-Morrissey rhetoric of the last five years is anything to go by, the opposite seems to be true. For despite the vast majority of his lyrical output (both solo and with The Smiths) expressing left-wing, inclusive, and progressive viewpoints, he seems not to be judged on what *they* 'stand for', but for what he says outside them, in interviews and web posts which, as Billy Bragg says suggest 'a commitment to a bigotry that tarnishes his persona as the champion of the outsider' (Roberts, 2019).

If, as we discussed earlier, the temptation is indeed to assume lyrics are a direct reflection of the lyricist, Morrissey's case would suggest that any such readings are trumped by our perceptions of them *outside* the words they are writing and/or singing.

All of this begs the age-old question of 'should we separate art from artist?' And, more pertinently to this discussion, 'should we judge an artist on their art or their life beyond it?' Lynskey suggests that one of the reasons the Morrissey situation has had such an impact is because the 'people who truly loved Morrissey did so because they felt that he understood them and shared their values, so their disappointment is unusually intense. When they fall out of love, they fall hard and there is no route back to that pure fandom' (Lynskey, 2017). Forming a personal connection with an artist can enhance our enjoyment of their music, but if that connection is then broken due to us taking issue with their behaviour (much like falling out with a friend because their political views don't chime with our own), it can irrevocably change our relationship with their music. In today's music industry, though, the artists themselves make it harder and harder to separate art from artist. As Baym says, 'today it's hard to even list all the sites where artists meet their audiences […] Facebook, Twitter […], Tumblr, Instagram, YouTube, Bandcamp,

Indaba, Snapchat, Line, Twitch, you name it' (Baym, 2018: 139), but with enormously successful acts like Taylor Swift's 'incredible success [...being] down to the relatability of her personality' (Clarke, 2023), solidifying the link between art and artist seems to be the preferred direction of most modern performers and is considered a risk worth taking, even if some may end up following Morrissey down the 'cancelled' route.

Wanting to get to know our favourite artists is nothing new, of course, and although it's easier in 2024 than in decades past to find out what they had for breakfast, or to get their take on the latest news story (assuming we accept these as theirs rather than their social media managers, that is) how we view them as *people* rather than as superstars has always been significant to their success. In the book *Exploring Personality and Performance in The Beatles* I note the role the Beatles' personalities played in their early success, with early British press praising their non-musical appeal, saying 'you have to be a real square not to love the nutty, noisy, happy, handsome Beatles' (Wardle, 2021) and, upon arriving in America, winning over 'a condescending press with knockabout charm and off-the-cuff wisecracks' (Beaumont, 2024). The Beatles' enormous popularity soon warranted a dedicated magazine, *The Beatles Book*, a slim monthly A5-sized magazine of around twenty-five pages which ran over seventy-seven issues between August 1963 and December 1969 (Fosbraey and Ash, 2022: 43) which granted their fans 'privileged access – visiting the group backstage, in the recording studio, in film sets and even in their homes' (Adams, 2015: Introduction). In the March 1964 edition of the magazine, Frederick James suggests that one of the (non-musical) reasons for the band's popularity is because of how grounded they were, noting their difference to 'the great stage, screen and disc stars of yesteryear' who were 'remote, far-off creatures perched upon high pedestals of pop glory [...] all sequins and gold lame with carefully created public images to reveal nothing more than small portions of their personalities' (Dean, 1963: 27). 'Can you imagine a Beatle putting up with that type of hypocrisy?' James, asks. 'Can you imagine a Beatle throwing a fit of temperament like some of the half-hysterical idols of past decades? Of course, you can't!' (Dean, 1963: 27). James also observes how much pleasure the band take in what they do, appearing to 'play and sing for their own personal pleasure [and that] their sights were set upon making their own music as a hobby rather than a job of work' (Dean, 1963: 27). We can see this reflected in the press coverage of the band from around this time, gathered in the book *Fifty Years with The Beatles* (Hill, 2012), where, through the photographs we are able to share in that collective joy, living vicariously through them. Even now, nearly sixty years on, it's hard to look at these images without smiling. On page 19, the four of them with their faces inches away from a Skaletrix set looking like they're about to burst with excitement; on page 23, John and Paul dancing out of the London Palladium; on page 26, laughing as they share a platter of cheese on cocktail sticks; page 33 mooning around with Morecombe and Wise, who look as overjoyed as they do; page 41, emerging from the plane to greet fans at JFK airport; page 47 splashing around in the sea in Florida. As photographer Robert Whitaker says in the book's introduction, fans 'were crazy about […] their energy and enthusiasm for life.' (Hill, 2012: 6). We'll never know if the quality of the Beatles' music alone would have made them the global phenomenon they became, but, as Beatles biographer Mark Lewisohn says, what made them extra special was due to how 'they did everything with down-to-earth humour, honesty, optimism, style, charisma, irreverence, intelligence and a particularly spiky disdain for falseness; how they were articulate, bold, curious, direct, instinctive, challenging, blunt, sharp, polite, rude, prickers of pomposity, rule-breakers never cowed by convention […and] created a profound and sustained connection to their public' (Lewisohn, 2013: x). None of which has anything to do with their music.

With the blueprint for fan engagement now set, bands (or their management teams) 'consciously cultivated their fan bases and tailored their image to create and bond together a group of supporters, often 'selling' an ideology to their fans to unite them' (Shepherd, 2003: 225). In recent years, the likes of 'Lady Gaga, Taylor Swift, and Lorde [… have resonated] with their fans through their music and public personas, an ability reinforced through contemporary social media' (Shuker, 2016: 78) with Swift further cementing the bond by speaking directly with her fans who she treats 'like friends' in an example of 'social media marketing extended to the hyper teenage BFF extreme' (Shuker, 2016: 74). Like with us hypothesising whether or not The Beatles would have been as popular without their lovable public image, it's impossible to say whether Swift would have had the same level of success had social media not existed, but it's clear that her 'talent goes beyond her music, spanning into the world of marketing, PR and branding' (HDK, 2024).

3.2. Music Video

Another way the artists can form a bond with their audience is through music video. Since the first music video aired on MTV in 1981 with 'the appropriately themed song' 'Video Killed The Radio Star', the format has been 'beneficial to developing artists' careers and promoting their music' (Hull et al., 2011: 270), and in 1992 'MTV began listing directors with the artist and song credits, reflecting the fact that music videos had increasingly become an artistic medium' (Eiss, 2013: 329). Music and music video are now so interlinked that it is often hard to imagine one existing without the other, and this was perhaps acknowledged in 2018 when it was announced that YouTube views would count towards the UK singles chart (Official Charts Company, 2018). I note in *Writing Song Lyrics* that 'there have [even] been numerous instances where a video has either led to the success of a song, or become MORE successful' (Fosbraey and Melrose, 2018: 69), so I suggest that in instances where a song has a music video attached to it and we have viewed it, the video becomes part of the overall 'text', and must therefore be considered when we analyse the song. In their introduction to the book *Music/ Video*, Arnold et al. even contend that music video be 'considered as either a new genre or addendum to music itself'(Arnold et al., 2019: 5). Although Watson and Railton write that 'all music videos have an avowedly commercial agenda: they are first and foremost a *commercial* for [...] the music track itself' (Railton and Watson, 2011: 2), they also note that '...the visual aspect of music video impacts upon [...] the meanings we can attach to [a song] and by extension how we can analyse and understand it' (Railton and Watson, 2011: 8).

In their book *Music Video and the Politics of Representation*, Railton and Watson break music video down into the different categories of 'Pseudo-Documentary'; 'Art'; 'Narrative'; and 'Staged Performance'.

A 'Pseudo-Documentary' music video apparently depicts the 'real life' of professional musicians (Railton and Watson, 2011: 49–51), which gives fans a 'glimpse into the off-stage stories and offer an "access all areas" account' (Garrigós & Ahonen, 2023: 234).

An 'Art' music video 'operates as a site of creative expression which variously works as an aesthetic complement to the song or vies with it for artistic consideration' (Railton and Watson, 2011: 51–52), with the likes of Sabrina Carpenter's 'Please Please Please' and Taylor Swift's 'Bad Blood' aesthetically complementing the lyrics, and Foo Fighter's 'Everlong' and OK Go's 'Here it Goes Again' vying with them for artistic consideration.

'Narrative' music videos can either function as a literal narration of the song (e.g. Aqua's 'Barbie Girl), or 'combine un-narrativised shots of the band performing the song [... with] a fictional diegesis that often works as an amplification of the story of the song (Railton and Watson, 2011: 57) (e.g. Magic's 'Rude').

The 'Staged Performance' music video doesn't 'offer an image of apparently unfettered reality' nor 'seek to tell a story [but...] exploits a performance that is explicitly staged for the production of the video' (Railton and Watson, 2011: 58) and we can see this in Daft Punk's 'Get Lucky' or Bon Jovi's 'Livin' on a Prayer'.

Which of these types of video an artist (or their management team) chooses informs us how they want to be represented to their audience. For their 2016 'Nothing Else Matters' music video, for example, Little Mix opt for the 'Pseudo-Documentary' style. The 'pseudo' prefix to the word 'documentary' here, however, tells us that what we are seeing isn't an *accurate* representation of the artist, but the representation of themselves they want to present to us. In the case of 'Nothing Else Matters', Little Mix want to appear as down-to-earth and relatable as possible, while also giving the impression that they're living their best lives with their best friends. The instrumental introduction of the song lasts for thirteen seconds, during which time the video moves through six different shots, all in black and white. In the first, we see the band in mid-shot, walking along a corridor towards the camera, chatting and laughing with one another as they go. In the second, we see a packed arena, with the lights from thousands of fans' phones illuminating the darkness. An elevated metal stage is visible above them. In the third, the camera shows a fan's view, off to the right and looking up of the stage at the four figures of Little Mix in mid-performance. The fourth shows a same-level central view of the band on stage, presumably the vantage point of fans in one of the upper tiers of the arena. Next, we are on the stage with the band, who we see via a long-shot, backs to us, singing out to the audience. This cuts to a mid-shot of the same, the band turn in unison to face the camera, and on fourteen seconds, Jade Thirlwall starts singing. These opening shots function in the same way an introduction to a formal essay might, setting up some background information (Little Mix are massively popular as they're playing to such a large crowd), laying out the intentions of what's to come (we're going to get an insider's perspective of the band), and establishing its main 'thesis statement' (the band members are fun-loving, united, and free from airs and graces, but also consummate professionals when it comes to putting on a show). To expand a little, then, let's examine how each shot leads to these assertions. If we pause shot 1 at the two-second mark, we see the following:

Jade raising her hands in the air in elation/celebration/ecstasy (take your pick, but the gesture is unmistakably positive and joyful);
Jesy and Perrie deep in excited conversation, with a beaming Leigh-Anne between them;
'Little Mix' written across the centre of the screen. The evolution of the band's 'logo' (their name) could be the focus of a detailed discussion it its own right, but for our purposes here, we just need to briefly note how it shifted from the coloured-crayon-esque 2011–2012 design, through 2012–2013's blocky, hot pink, to this one, a marker-pen scrawl, which was used between 2013 and 2018. We can see here how the designs represent the

different stages of the band: playful and almost child-like to reflect the band's youth and inexperience (while also making it clear who their target audience was); eye-catching, bold, and generally difficult to ignore to seize upon their early success and cement themselves in people's minds; more reserved, but with the effect of spontaneity, with the logo now looking like it's a signature from one (or, somehow, *all*) of the band members. Now a successful act, with no more need for establishing fan demographic or attention-grabbing, the band's focus is now to hold onto the loyal fans they've attracted, so relatability, accessibility, and authenticity are the order of the day. A logo which gives the impression it's been hand-written rather than manufactured, is therefore exactly what's required. 'So', thinks the tweenage schoolkid, 'this is a band of normal people *just like us*, who have a logo we can easily copy into our school notebooks with a Sharpie.' Because that's how they came up with it themselves, right?

A corridor. In a few seconds, we'll see the arena which will enable us to backtrack and make the connection that the corridor is 'back-stage', but at this point, the only visual clue we have for such is the distinctive roadcase (heavy-duty boxes used for transporting music equipment). The important thing is the ordinariness of their surroundings, and the fact they are there alone, sans bodyguards, managers, PR team, backing dancers, etc. It's just the four of them, happy to be in each-other's company (maybe that's *all* they need to be happy?), glamorous themselves with full make-up and carefully styled hair, completely unconcerned by their unglamorous surroundings, which with the breeze-blocked, undecorated walls, stacked tables and chairs, and fluorescent lighting could even be a school corridor if we don't see the roadcase. Seeing them in this seemingly unguarded, natural way, excitedly interacting with one another as they (we presume) make their way to the stage, gives us a privileged insider's perspective.

When we contrast this first shot with the next five, then, we are invited to wonder how the band members can be so down-to-earth when they're adored by thousands upon thousands of people. And this is where our 'thesis statement' comes in where the band members are fun-loving, united, and free from airs and graces (as we see from the first shot), but consummate professionals when it comes to putting on a show (as we see from the subsequent five shots). The 'professionalism' is key here, not just because it contrasts with the informality of the first shot, but because it shows us that they respect their fans; that they make an effort for them by getting dressed up, making their shows visually appealing, learning complex choreography, and singing live. An argument could be made that the model for how a band should present themselves was created by Brian Epstein in January 1962 when he signed The Beatles, a leather-clad 'gang of thugs' (The Beatles, 2000: 73) who smoked, ate, drank, and wrestled on stage, belched into the microphone, and made V-signs at their audience (Norman, 2004: 140). By the time they recorded their debut album little over a year later, Epstein had turned this 'group of Liverpool hard rockers into a prototypical Boy Band' (Savage, 2023), making them disciplined, professional, polite, and an act 'that could be embraced by boys and girls, men and women, people of all ages and ethnicities' (Tiwary, 2014).

We should also include the colour (or lack of) in our analysis. Filmed entirely in black-and-white, it is clear that 'Nothing Else Matters' is presenting us with something very different from the previous month's 'Shout Out To My Ex', which, journalist Qianqian Yang says, is a 'not-so-subtle tutorial on how to step up your Instagram game' where the best content involves 'unconventional colors [sic], fake laughs, and good lighting' (Yang, 2016). Black-and-white has long been associated 'with realism' (Asimow and Mader, 2004: 113) as well as giving audiences 'a sense of authenticity' (Ban, 1998: 82). It's can also be, as Präkel says, 'more powerful' than colour as it 'simplifies and produces a new clarity by [...] removing colour to leave only tone. It is like taking away the skin to reveal the musculature, bone and sinews beneath' (Präkel, 2008: 10–11). As a Pseudo-Documentary music video, 'Nothing Else Matters' wants to appear real and authentic, and, it seems, filming it in black-and-white is a shortcut to achieving this. If we go a little further into the video, we can also see that Präkel's observation about black-and-white showing us what's under the surface is also applicable. Interspersed with shots of the band on the metal stage is supposedly candid behind-the-scenes footage of them learning dance routines (dressed in everyday clothing like tracksuit bottoms and baggy hoodies), travelling to the venue, getting hair and make-up ready for the show, and having lots of hugs – with their mothers, fans, and each other. Lyrically, the song is a paint-by-numbers account of a couple who despite their arguments find that 'nothing else matters' except for their love for one another. Fitting this against the visuals of the music video would seem like a tall order, and, indeed, much of it is inapplicable, but director Adam Goodall and his editing team makes an asset out of the lines 'we've come so far' and 'nothing else matters like us', switching their meanings in the process. With the three utterances of 'we've come so far', we see: 1. the band practising a dance routine in the aforementioned tracksuit bottoms and hoodies (*suggesting, when it comes to performing the routine in the arena, how far they'd have come from this point*); 2. Perrie and Leigh-Anne climbing a hill then pointing toward a cityscape at its peak (*a more literal interpretation of the phrase*); and 3. posing for photographs with fans in front of a banner advertising

'Now 104.3 Vegas' New Music Channel' (*look how far they've come in their careers, posing for adoring fans in Las Vegas*). The line 'Nothing else matters like us', is sung four times, alongside these scenes: 1. The band, all together, on stage, laughing hysterically in a toilet, and hugging in their dressing room (the 'us'; referring to their band unity); 2. Shots of screaming fans (the 'us' now expanded to include them); 3. The band on stage with backing dancers (who are now, we are told, part of the 'us' unit), and 4. Shots of band, backing dancers, and fans (bringing all elements of the 'us' together).

To draw all of this together, 'the Nothing else matters' video shows us that Little Mix have a great relationship with one another, are hardworking, down-to-earth, fun-loving, family-oriented, appreciate their fans, backing dancers, and success, and are living lives every bit as wonderful as the media tells us they're supposed to be. A Jesy Nelson interview following her exit from the band in 2021 reminds us of the 'Pseudo' part of 'Pseudo-Documentary', though, with her suggesting things weren't as idyllic as the images the video as presenting us with. 'Being in a girl band, you are a machine going all the time', she said, 'You don't have a minute to breathe and take time out if you just need space. That was something I struggled with. For me my mental health issues were an ongoing thing while I was in Little Mix. I was struggling with my body issues, I was constantly being trolled – and I really, really struggled with it' (Hirwani, 2023). To show these struggles in the 'Nothing Else Matters' video wouldn't have presented the image that the band were trying to put across at the time, though, of course.

In her book *Experiencing Music Video: Aesthetics and Cultural Context*, Vernallis writes that 'in a music video both the song and the image play shifting roles in articulating the lyrics. The image can render certain words more obscure and others more apparent. If we look closely, we notice that, like other elements, lyrics can come to the fore for a moment and then fade away. The lyrics fragment, and thus they become mysterious and unreachable' (Vernallis 2004: xiii). In *Reading Eminem*, I discuss how, in the case of the song 'Stan', the music video changes the way we might read the song as it visually attaches the words of Dido's sung sections to Stan's girlfriend, who is played in the video by Dido herself. 'If we look only at the song, and ignore the music video, the girlfriend is not given a voice at all, and we are more inclined simply to attach Dido's voice straight to Stan, who we find out is struggling with mental illness,' (Fosbraey, 2022b: 66), so how we interpret the song depends on whether or not we have seen the music video.

Via an analysis of the Eminem song 'Headlights' I also demonstrate how music videos can intensify or elevate the listener's emotional connection with the lyrics. 'Headlights' achieves this 'by bringing a different viewpoint into the song, literally in this case, because we see most of the footage from the perspective of Eminem's mother, Debbie' (Fosbraey, 2022b: 69). Not only is this alternative viewpoint present in the video, but it also achieves a full narrative arc for Debbie, with a complete set of 'story elements' present:

> 'The **status quo**, 'the position of the main character at the start of the story' (Willett, 2013: 34), which shows Debbie, our main character in this music video, struggling for money, living alone, constantly reminded of the rich and famous son who disowned her [...]
>
> The **inciting incident**, where Debbie decides to reach out to Eminem but is rejected (to the extent where she can't [sic] even get past the security guards where he lives)
>
> Her **desire** to rekindle her relationship with him, shown through her reminiscing about him as a child via the photo album and the memories that come from it.
>
> The **crisis** where she mistakes a man in the park for Eminem, then returns home, alone, to get drunk and destroys her Christmas tree and decorations in anger and frustration, believing she'll [sic] never be able to repair their relationship.
>
> The **climax** where she manages to see Eminem and they embrace. and the **resolution** where she receives the lyrics to this song in the post, which see Eminem apologising to her and telling her he loves her. This leads to Debbie being able to find peace, and the video ends with her looking through the photo album again, closing it as the line 'I want a new life' (Eminem, 2013a) plays, suggesting she is now able to move on' (Fosbraey, 2022b: 71–72).

After this analysis, I go on to discuss how some videos introduce a different or additional *concept* into the overall song narrative, and I use the music video for 'When I'm Gone' as example. In this video, 'the first minute is dedicated to setting up a context for the confessional content of the lyrics. In a narrative which is not present in the lyrics, we are shown a small gathering of people, sitting in what appears to be a school gymnasium, listening to a man finish a speech at a lectern [...] The event's organiser then steps up the lectern, inviting someone else to "share" with the group. Eminem stands, makes his way to the podium, and after introducing himself as "Marshall" gives a Pinter-sized pause before launching into the song's lyrics. In retrospect, with our subsequent knowledge of Eminem's drug dependency, it does not take much of a stretch to imagine this event as some kind of group therapy meeting' (Fosbraey, 2022b: 72–73), a concept which we do not find within the lyrics themselves.

As well as functioning as ways to enhance the narrative appeal of songs, however, there are drawbacks to the power of the music video format, which I explore in the section 'Girl Power?' of *Viva Hate* where I 'highlight the double standards between how men and women are treated in the industry' (Fosbraey, 2022a: 13), focusing particularly on how women are depicted in music video. Austerlitz writes that 'videos live and die on the presentation of women as ready, luscious, and able, always unclothed, often nubile, and unquestioningly present as objects of male desire' (Austerlitz, 2007: 5). I analyse the music videos output of a range of female performers, noting that not only are the vast majority of these literally operating under the male gaze of a male director, but are also constructed to satisfy what Kristin Lieb says are 'sexual fantasies (and fantasy types)' for heterosexual men (Lieb, 2018: 120). This ranges from the 'erotic magic of high heels' (Jeffreys, 2005: 139) which female artists are expected to wear, through to the female–female–male 'threesome', which is 'the top male sexual fantasy according to a poll by "sexual wellness experts" *Sinful* (Glover, 2022). Female performers are 'held to rigid standards of appearance' (Lieb, 2018: 9) and their images 'seem to be more important commodities than the music they write and perform' (McCallum and Dzidic, 2019: 405) and this often leads to songs with no discernible sexual content being sexualised in their music videos in order to perpetuate such behaviours. Examples are too numerous to list, but include Little Mix's 'Sweet Melody', Dua Lipa and Miley Cyrus's 'Prisoner', and Britney Spears' 'Toxic'.

3.3. Album Art

'Hard copy' music also brings with it an influence beyond the music itself. I observe in *Viva Hate* that 'although an album is essentially a musical medium, it is also a multimodal product' (Fosbraey, 2022a: 58–59), and if we are receiving it in a physical medium, we are exposed to non-music elements such as the album cover artwork, any other artwork (including booklets, back covers, and spines), the lyric transcripts (if included), acknowledgments, credits, record label information, and copyright and publishing details. As we are a visual people, and, as Berger notes, 'Seeing comes before words. The child looks and recognizes before it can speak' (Berger, 1972: 7) the importance of such factors must not be overlooked when thinking about the overall listening experience.

I write in *Viva Hate* that 'as well as considering what album covers mean to us personally, they can also be analysed in the same way that we might analyse a piece of text, looking for symbols, messages, and meanings' (Fosbraey, 2022a: 59). Drawing upon Roland Barthes' 'Rhetoric of the Image' which presents us with a strategy on how to 'read' a photograph or picture in order to uncover its 'message' (Barthes, 1977: 36), I conducted a detailed analysis of the artwork in NWA's *Straight Outta Compton*, 'approaching it […] as if we were walking into a record store in 1988 and picking it up for the first time' (Fosbraey, 2022a: 59). This requires us to pay close attention to whatever is available to us visually 'decode' it, and in the case of *Straight Outta Compton* it means we are able to use the front and back cover images, album title, the group name, song titles, and a 'parental advisory explicit content' label to uncover what Barthes calls the 'three messages', which are 'a linguistic message, a coded iconic message, and a non-coded iconic message' (Barthes, 1977: 36). With regard to the linguistic message Barthes says its function is to '"anchor" the spectrum of possible meanings, by selecting some interpretations and securing the intended meaning' (Mocini, 2005: 153) and that 'the linguistic level fixes the floating chain of signifiers in such a way as to counter the terror of uncertain signs' (Barthes, 1964: 37). Berger goes even further in stressing the importance of any words that appear with the images, saying that 'the photograph begs for an interpretation, and the words usually supply it. The photograph, irrefutable as evidence but weak in meaning, is given a meaning by the words' (Berger, 2013: 66).

In my analysis, as well as the aforementioned album title, group name, song titles, and 'parental advisory explicit content' sticker, we also have visible text 'via Eazy-E, Ice Cube, and MC Ren, who all wear Los Angeles Raiders baseball caps, and DJ Yella, who wears an LA Lakers jacket' (Fosbraey, 2022a: 62). This may seem like a small matter, but actually offers a significant social commentary. As I write: 'The Los Angeles Raiders were based in Oakland at the time, a city which had a 46.9% black population in 1980 and 43.9% in 1990 (compared with Los Angeles itself which showed figures of 17% in 1980 and 14% in 1990). In the LA Raiders, N.W.A. had 'found a kindred spirit' (Alipour, 2010). Says Ice Cube: 'we're the Raiders. We're pirates, which was our attitude […] They moved to our backyard […] They moved the baddest team with the baddest attitude into one of the baddest cities in America. It convinced the world that this kind of LA really exists' (Alipour, 2010). They were also 'the team NFL fans loved to hate' (Caldwell, 2021), presenting an underdog, 'us against the world' aesthetic that mirrored that of N.W.A themselves. Just this small linguistic message, then, gives us access to something much broader' (Fosbraey, 2022a: 62).

Overall, 'the group name, album title, parental advisory sticker, LA Raiders text on the baseball caps, and song titles […] work with the images to lead us to the following: A group of men from a neighbourhood with a large black population who have been racially discriminated against, possibly for their whole lives, and subjected to 'racial profiling and police brutality' (Oware, 2018: 3), decide to fight back at the forces who have abused them. Now in the position of complete power, they subvert the violence and hatred they have faced, and turn it on the perpetrator, becoming the haters, rather than the hated' (Fosbraey, 2022a: 66). And all of this without reading a single lyric or hearing a single note of music. When we *do* listen, it's evident that the artwork is making a 'statement in relation to the style of music' (Shuker, 2016: 82) contained on the album, and is functioning as a visual representation of its lyrical content.

Album art can also function as a way to enhance the songs' storytelling, and in the sub-chapter 'Album art: the CD booklet and storytelling' in *Reading Eminem* I explore how on studio albums *The Eminem Show* and *Encore*, and the Greatest Hits collection *Curtain Call*, Eminem uses 'the CD booklet to tell visual stories, almost like the comics he loved so much as a child' (Fosbraey, 2022b: 62), creating a three-part narrative through image alone. *The Eminem Show*'s artwork 'sets up a story whereby Eminem feels his every move is scrutinised and his life has become a 'show'. *Encore* continues this, with Eminem disillusioned so much by this that he kills his audience (and, importantly, shoots straight at the camera killing the gaze of the audience outside the theatre), then kills himself. *Curtain Call* then completes this visual narrative [...with its] front cover [... aping] the cover of [*Encore* with a] besuited Eminem on a stage', but with the booklet working as a retrospective of the roles the 'dead' Eminem has played in his lyrics, showing him alternatively as 'the 'ordinary' person'; 'the sex symbol'; 'the victim', 'the tortured artist'; and as the 'dangerous'' (Fosbraey, 2022b: 63), all roles he has taken on within his lyrics.

According to Barthes, text on an image 'constitutes what he calls a parasitic message, designed to quicken the reading with additional signifiers' (Crow, 2011: 74). In the case of *The Marshall Mathers LP 2* the disproportionately large number '2' in the middle of the album title on the front cover signifies that we consider this the second part of something, and therefore invites us to include the *first* part, *The Marshall Mathers LP* in order to form a complete reading.

On the cover of [...] *LP*, Eminem sits on the steps of his childhood home, as the house itself, ominously half in shadow, looms over him. In an interview, Mathers tells us 'that was the house that I grew up in my teenage years. One day I dreamt of being able to go back to that house and remember everything that I went through. I thought, "What if I did the cover at my old house sitting on the steps like I used to do?" That would be so crazy to me. We did it and I guess I made my house famous' (VH1, 2000). Although comparatively small in the image compared to the house, the fact he is looking directly at us makes him automatically makes him 'the focal point' (Rowse, 2024) and also makes us 'more emotionally connected to the picture' (Kim, 2024). On [...] *LP 2*'s cover, Mathers is absent, so the focal point shifts to the house, which, shot from below and without the presence of Mathers 'holds power over the viewer' and appears 'very intimidating' (NYFA, 2023). Whereas on the cover of [...] *LP* the house looked in decent condition, with neat awning over the front stoop, a metal security gate ahead of the front door, a security light adjacent, nicely framed windows, and a clean, in-tact drainpipe, in [...] *LP 2*, the awning, gate, light, and drainpipe are all gone, and the windows and front door are boarded up. The bottoms of the images are also different. In [...] *LP*, the photograph ends almost directly under the front steps, but in [...] *LP 2* there is a fair amount of foreground before we get to the steps, showing a mess of weeds and overgrown shrubbery which also extends round the side of the house, where brittle, dead branches stretch midway up the ground floor windows. The overall effect is one of dilapidation; that in the thirteen years between shots, the house has fallen into such a state of disrepair that it's now uninhabitable. This is compounded by [...] *LP 2*'s back cover, which shows a sign from the City of Detroit condemning it. In his chapter 'The visual availability of culture' Ball comments that photographs of buildings 'serve as documents which stand on behalf of the circumstances they visually depicts' (Ball, 2005: 128). In its current condition, combined with the with the cover of [...] *LP* and the knowledge that it's Eminem's childhood home, it's clear that the circumstances being visually depicted are that: a significant amount of time has passed between [...] *LP* and *LP2*, and a significant amount of change has also occurred, but below the surface (and below the weeds and boarded-up windows), things are still the same. From there, it's not too much of a stretch for us to see [...] *LP2's* cover as a signifier that Mathers' past still weighs heavily on him. When we listen to the album, we see this reading borne out in lyrics such as: 'It's like 'I'm in this dirt, digging up old hurt', 'I'm coming for closure', and 'here we go all over again' (from 'Bad Guy') (Eminem, 2013); 'Cut the fucking act like you're happy, I'm fucking back again/ With another anthem, why stop when it doesn't have to end?' ('Survival') (Eminem, 2013) 'Got it all, but I still won't change' and 'I can't even help it, this is the hand I was dealt/ a creature of habit, feel like I'm trapped' ('So Far[...]') (Eminem, 2013); 'I want a new life (start over)/ One without a cause (clean slate)' and 'I guess we are who we are' ('Headlights') (Eminem, 2013); and 'still Shady inside, hair every bit as dyed' ('Evil Twin') (Eminem, 2013).

We saw in Section 2 that the value of spending time 'inside the song', but in the vast majority of instances, this only presents us with part of the story. Unless music has been created and released in a vacuum, with no available information on the artist, no marketing, no music video, and no artwork, then it is crucial that we consider what is going on beyond the confines of the song itself. The moment any of these external factors are released into the world, they *become* part of the overall text and must not be ignored if we're going to form a comprehensive analysis.

Chapter 4

CONCLUSION

Although it may be the case, as Gans notes, that 'historically, classical music and avant-garde music have been viewed as [the] "high culture" formats' (Gans, 2010: 86, 172) and that 'many words have been written dismissing the pop song lyric as 'disposable – or worse, as spiritually bankrupt' (Frisicks-Warren, 2006: 2), one only needs to conduct a quick Google Images search of 'Song Lyric tattoos' to see how important popular music is to people. I begin the book *Composing Song Lyrics* by noting how, as well as being permanently inked onto people's skin, lyrics have been used to express sentiment and emotion at key points (e.g. to express feelings of love and unity at weddings or sadness and loss at funerals), have been cited in suicide notes and court cases, and even, in the case of Tyler The Creator, used as ammunition by a government to deny entry to the UK. I expand upon this in the sub-chapter 'Why not just write instrumentals?' where I draw upon a quote from international speaker and author Yehuda Berg that says 'words are singularly the most powerful force available to humanity', observing that 'if we combine the power of words with the power of music, it leads us to a combination that brings meaning, hope, passion, enlightenment, wonder and humour to millions of people every year' (Fosbraey & Melrose, 2019: xiii). 'Instrumental music' I go on to say, 'can entertain us; it can make us feel emotion; it can allow us to reflect; it can even persuade us to physically react by dancing or grimacing or smiling. But though there may be a melody in existence that we can say "sums up our lives", the addition of words persuades us of a certain viewpoint or makes us re-evaluate our outlook on life; or can make us laugh or feel disgusted or like we're not alone. Lyrics can achieve all of these things and more' (Fosbraey & Melrose, 2019: xiii). I conclude this section of the book by observing how lyrics, although 'tolerant both of banality and repetition […] of filler syllables […] of meaninglessness, too' (Leith, 2007), can convey complex and important messages that melody alone cannot, citing John Lennon's 'Give peace a chance', Plan B's 'Ill Manors' and Rage Against the Machine's 'Killing in the Name' as examples, discussing as they do, peace, political disquiet, elitism, and police brutality, respectively.

Whatever a lyricist's intentions, though, regardless of whether they were trying to be intellectual, sophisticated, or captivating, or simply writing lyrics because that's what the popular music format requires, what must be considered is how their words are received by the public. As Noel Gallagher once said when asked what the lyrics to the Oasis song 'Champagne Supernova' meant: 'I don't fucking know [...] but are you telling me, when you've got 60,000 people singing it, they don't know what it means? It means something different to every one of them' (Hogan, 2010).

In a variety of forms and approaches, I have explored how lyrics, music video, and album art can work together to form what Duffett defines as 'transmedia storytelling', which is 'the process of telling different parts of the same story through different electronic media' (Duffett, 2013: 12) and, indeed, the benefits of doing so. Inspired by Hopps' assertions (after Barthes) that we should move away from relying on the lyricist's intentions when discerning meaning within a song, my work has also shifted the focus from the lyricist to elements of language, character, and narrative, and in so doing, given popular music the same kind of attention we might afford to literature, poetry, or film.

Overall, it has been my aim to resituate and repurpose existing theoretical techniques to function within the field of popular music analysis while also introducing techniques of my own. In doing this, I feel I have presented a way to examine this ever-changing and ever-influential format in a way that befits its importance. Bill Frisicks-Warren writes that 'ours is a world in which great numbers of people look to pop music [...] for guidance that conventional religious observance does not provide' (Frisicks-Warren, 2006: 228). A touch hyperbolic, perhaps, but to those of us who find that quote resonates, even just a bit, there will always be a desire to keep researching and keep writing about this medium we love so much. In my own small way, I hope I have added to and moved forward the constantly evolving world of popular music criticism.

REFERENCES

Adams, T. (2015). *Looking Through You: The Beatles Book Monthly photo archive*. London: Omnibus Press.
Aitkenhead, D. (2011). '2011: the year in review'. https://www.theguardian.com/uk/2011/dec/30/2011-end-of-year-review (accessed 24 November 2024).
Alipour, S. (2022). 'Ice Cube talks film and his Raiders'. http://www.espn.com/espn/page2/story?id=5120507 (accessed 24 March 2023).
Allen, G. (2000). *Intertextuality*. Abingdon: Routledge.
Allen, G. (2011). *Intertextuality (second edition)*. Abingdon: Routledge.
Armstrong, E.G. (2004). 'Eminem's Construction of Authenticity'. *Popular Music and Society, 27*(3), 335–355. https://doi.org/10.1080/03007760410001733170.
Arnold, G., Cookney, D., Fairclough, K., & Goddard, M. (eds.) (2019). *Music/Video*. London: Bloomsbury.
Asimow, M., Mader, S. (2004). *Law and Popular Culture: A Course Book*. Austria: Peter Lang.
Astor, P. (2010). 'The poetry of rock: song lyrics are not poems but the words still matter; another look at Richard Goldstein's collection of rock lyrics'. *Popular Music, 29*(1), 143–148.
Axis of Awesome. (2011). '4 Chords'. https://www.youtube.com/watch?v=oOlDewpCfZQ (accessed 1 December 2024).
Aune, D. E. (2003). *The Westminster Dictionary of New Testament and Early Christian Literature and Rhetoric*. United Kingdom: Presbyterian Publishing Corporation.
Ball, M. 'The visual availability of culture'. (2005). In: Prosser, J. (ed.) *Image-based Research: A Sourcebook for Qualitative Researchers*. United Kingdom: Taylor & Francis.
Ban, K. C. (1998). *The Silent Word: Textual Meaning and the Unwritten*. Singapore: Singapore University Press, National University of Singapore.
Barnet, S., & Cain, W. E. (2005). *A Short Guide to Writing about Literature*. New York: Pearson/Longman.
Barthes, R., 1964, *'Éléments de sémiologie'*. London: Cape.
Barthes, R. (1977). *Image, Music, Text*. London: Fontana Press.
Little Bastard. (2012). 'A re-introduction to Plan B'. http://www.polarimagazine.com/features/re-introduction-plan-b/ (accessed 3 December 2024).
Bate, C. (2023). "A Shakespearean in love with Taylor Swift; Sir Jonathan Bate is a world authority on the Bard – and a long-time fanboy of the American singer. Here, he shall compare her (favourably) to the giants of literature." *Sunday Times* [London, England], 9 Apr. 2023, p. 18. *Gale OneFile: News*, link.gale.com/apps/doc/A744821745/STND?u=ucwinch&sid=bookmark-STND&xid=e61def3c (accessed 26 April 2023).
Bate, D. (2016). *Photography*. London: Bloomsbury.
Baym, N. K. (2018). *Playing To The Crowd*. New York: New York University Press.

BBC News. (2006). 'Cameron defends 'hoodie' speech'. http://news.bbc.co.uk/1/hi/uk_politics/5163798.stm (accessed 5 December 2024).

BBC News. (2010). 'Tuition fees vote: Plans approved despite rebellion'. https://www.bbc.co.uk/news/uk-politics-11952449 (accessed 2 December 2024).

Beaumont, M. (2024). 'Crazed girls, loose bladders, and JFK: How The Beatles defied the odds to break America'. https://www.independent.co.uk/arts-entertainment/music/features/the-beatles-america-fans-b2491382.html (accessed 2 December 2024).

Beard, A. (2001). *Texts and Contexts*. London: Routledge.

Bell, B. (2021). 'Riots 10 years on: The five summer nights when London burned'. https://www.bbc.co.uk/news/uk-england-london-58058031 (accessed 2 December 2024).

Bender, D. E. (2011). *American Abyss: Savagery and Civilization in the Age of Industry*. United States: Cornell University Press.

Bennett, A., Shank, B., & Toynbee, J. (eds.). (2006). *The Popular Music Studies Reader*. London: Routledge.

Bennett, J. (2012a). 'Everything you ever wanted to know about the word 'chav''. https://www.birmingham.ac.uk/accessibility/transcripts/dr-joe-bennett-chav (accessed 3 December 2024).

Bennett, J. (2012b). Chav-spotting in Britain: the representation of social class as private choice. *Social Semiotics*. https://doi.org/10.1080/10350330.2012.708158.

Berger, J. (1972) *Ways of Seeing*. London: Penguin.

Berger, J. (2013). *Understanding a Photograph*. London: Penguin.

Bickford, T. (2007). Music of Poetry and Poetry of Song: Expressivity and Grammar in Vocal Performance. *Ethnomusicology, 51*(3), 439–476. http://www.jstor.org/stable/20174545.

Bicknell, J. (2009). *Why Music Moves Us*. United Kingdom: Palgrave Macmillan UK.

Birrell, I. (2012). 'Don't mock 'hug a hoodie'. It was, and still is, the right message'. https://www.theguardian.com/commentisfree/2012/may/31/hug-a-hoodie-cameron-prison (accessed 5 December 2024).

Blair, H. (1814). *Lectures on Rhetoric and Belles Lettres*. United Kingdom: Largin & Thompson.

Blanton, S. (2010). *The Songwriter's Toolkit: From Pen to Push Play*. United States: Tate Publishing & Enterprises, LLC.

Blonsky, M. (ed.) (1985). *On Signs: A Semiotics Reader*. Oxford: Basil Blackwell.

Bloomsbury. (2017). 'Music as Multimodal Discourse'. https://www.bloomsbury.com/uk/music-as-multimodal-discourse (accessed 22 November 2024).

Blume, J. (2004). *Steps to songwriting Success*. New York. Billboard Books.

Booker, Christopher (2004). *The Seven Basic Plots: Why We Tell Stories*. London: Continuum.

Boombox. 'Eminem. Zane Lowe. Part 3'. https://theboombox.com/eminem-zane-lowe-interview-part-3/ (accessed 22 November 2024).

Booth, W. C. (1961). *The Rhetoric of Fiction*. London: The University of Chicago Press.

Booth, W. C. (2004). *The Rhetoric of RHETORIC*. Oxford: Blackwell.

Borchers, T. & Hundley, H. (2018). *Rhetorical Theory: An Introduction*, Second Edition. Illinois: Waveland Press.

Botelho, C. M., & de Lemos Martins, M. "Suddenly, Hope": Semiotic Analysis of a News Magazine Front Cover, *The Economist*.

Botha, M. (2016) 'Microction.', in *The Cambridge Companion to the English Short Story*. Cambridge: Cambridge University Press, pp. 201–220. Cambridge companions to literature. http://dro.dur.ac.uk/22834/1/22834.pdf.

REFERENCES

Braun, R. (2008). *Constructing Authorship in the Work of Günter Grass*. United Kingdom: OUP Oxford.
Brackett, D. (1995). *Interpreting Popular Music*. Cambridge: Cambridge University Press.
Bradley, A. & DuBois, A. (eds.). (2010). *The Anthology of Rap*. New Haven: Yale University Press.
Brook, P. (2017). *Tip of the Tongue: Reflections on Language and Meaning*. London: Nick Hern Books.
Brown, J. (2011). 'On Cameron's 'hug a hoodie' estate, Big Society has made little impact'. https://www.independent.co.uk/news/uk/politics/on-cameron-s-hug-a-hoodie-estate-big-society-has-made-little-impact-2366159.html (accessed 5 December 2024).
Burroway, J. (2007). *Imaginative Writing: The Elements of Craft* (2nd edition) (New York: Penguin Academics).
Butler, C. (2020). 'Unaware of voters' preferences: the Liberal Democrats' notorious U-turn on tuition fees'. https://blogs.lse.ac.uk/politicsandpolicy/libdems-tuition-fees/ (accessed 3 December 2024).
Bryant, G. A. (2011). Verbal irony in the wild. *Pragmatics & Cognition*, 19(2), 291–309.
Byrne, D. (2012). *How Music Works*. Edinburgh: Canongate.
Caldwell, D. (2021). 'The Raiders are dangerously close to NFL relevance again'. https://www.theguardian.com/sport/2021/sep/29/the-raiders-are-dangerously-close-to-nfl-relevance-again (accessed 26 March 2023).
Callahan, M. (2005). *The Trouble with Music*. Edinburgh: AK Press.
Christmann, G. B. (2008, September). 'The power of photographs of buildings in the Dresden urban discourse. Towards a visual discourse analysis.' In: *Forum Qualitative Sozialforschung/Forum: Qualitative Social Research* (Vol. 9, No. 3).
Clark, J. S. (1891). *A Briefer Practical Rhetoric*. United States: H. Holt.
Clarke, N. (2023). 'Taylor Swift: What makes the singer so popular?' https://www.standard.co.uk/culture/music/taylor-swift-south-america-australia-asia-brits-b1099976.html (accessed 6 January 2024).
Clifton, K. (2004). 'Queer hearing and the Madonna Queen'. In: Fouz-Hernandez, S. & Jarman-Ivens, F. (eds.). *Madonna's Drowned Worlds*. Aldershot: Ashgate.
Cobain, K. (2003). *Journals*. London: Penguin.
Cocker, J. (2011). *Mother, Brother, Lover: Selected Lyrics*. United Kingdom: Faber & Faber.
Collini, S. (ed.) (1992). *Umberto Eco: Interpretation and overinterpretation*. Cambridge: Cambridge University Press.
Costello, E. (2015). *Unfaithful Music and Disappearing Ink*. London: Viking.
Cragg, M. (2012). 'Plan B ill Manors Review'. https://www.bbc.co.uk/music/reviews/p9zb/ (accessed 7 December 2024).
Cross, C. R. (2002). *Heavier than Heaven*. London: Hodder and Stoughton.
Crow, D. (2011). *Visible Signs (Second Edition): An Introduction to Semiotics in the Visual Arts*. Switzerland: Bloomsbury Academic.
Crowded House, (1986). 'Don't Dream It's Over'. In: *Crowded House* [CD]. Capitol; EMI.
Csathy, P. (2021). 'The Story Behind Crowded House's "Hey Now, Hey Now" Anthem "Don't Dream It's Over"'. https://consequence.net/2021/12/crowded-house-dont-dream-its-over-story-behind-the-song (accessed 1 December 2024).
Cubitt, G. (2007). *History and Memory*. Manchester: Manchester University Press.
Culpeper, J. (2011). *Impoliteness: Using Language to Cause Offence*. Cambridge: Cambridge University Press.
Curtin, B. (2009). 'Semiotics and visual representation'. *Semantic Scholar*, 51–62.

Curtis, D. and Savage, J. (eds.). (2014). *So this is Permanence: Ian Curtis*. London: Faber and Faber.
Cyprus Mail (2016), '"Greatest living poet" Bob Dylan wins Nobel literature prize'. *Cyprus Mail [Cyprus]*, 13 October, available: https://link.gale.com/apps/doc/A466630574/STND?u=ucwinch&sid=bookmark-STND&xid=3d628fb4 (accessed 26 April 2023).
Damon, M., & Livingston, I. (eds.). (2009). *Poetry and Cultural Studies: A Reader*. University of Illinois Press.
Dane, J. A. (2011). *The Critical Mythology of Irony*. Greece: University of Georgia Press.
Dansby, A, (2003). 'Judge drops Eminem rap'. https://www.rollingstone.com/music/music-news/judge-drops-eminem-rap-183834/ (accessed 30 August 2020).
Dean, J. (ed.). (1963). *Beatles Book Issue 4*. Beat Monthly Publications.
Denora, T. (2006). 'Music and Self Identity'. In: Bennett, A., Shank, B., & Toynbee, J. (eds). *The Popular Music Studies Reader*. United Kingdom: Routledge.
Dibben, N. (2009). *Bjork*. Bloomington and Indianapolis: Indiana University Press.
Dillane, A. Power, M.J., Devereux, E., & Haynes, A. (2018). *Songs of Social Protest*. London: Rowman & Littlefield.
Dimery, R. (ed.). (2013). *1001 Songs You Must Hear Before You Die*. London: Quintessence.
Dolley, C., Walford, R. (2015). *The One-Act Play Companion: A Guide to Plays, Playwrights and Performance*. United Kingdom: Bloomsbury Publishing.
Dooley, R, (2011). 'Personality C/L/A/S/H'. In: *Clash, November 2011*.
Draper, J. (2008). *A Brief History of Album Covers*. London: Flame Tree Publishing.
Drew, S., & Guillemin, M. (2014). From photographs to findings: Visual meaning-making and interpretive engagement in the analysis of participant-generated images. Visual Studies, 29(1), 54–67.
duChemin, D. (2009). *Within the Frame: The Journey of Photographic Vision*. Pearson Education.
Duffett, M. (2013). *Understanding Fandom*. London: Bloomsbury.
Dworkin, A. (1974). *Woman Hating*. New York: E.P Dutton.
Echard, W. (2005). *Neil Young and the Poetics of Energy*. Bloomington: Indiana University Press.
Eckstein, L. (2010). *Reading Song Lyrics*. Amsterdam: Rodopi.
Edwards, P. (2009). *How to Rap*. Chicago: Chicago Review Press.
Eels. (2024). '*Eels: Blinking Lights and Other Revelations*'. https://eelstheband.com/eels_blinkinglights.php (accessed 26 November 2024).
Eiss, H. (2013). *Mythology of Dance*. United Kingdom: Cambridge Scholars Publishing.
Eminem. (1999). 'Brain Damage'. In: *The Slim Shady LP* [CD]. Interscope; Aftermath.
Eminem. (2000). *Angry Blonde*. New York: Regan Books.
Eminem. (2000a). 'The Way I am'. In: *The Marshal Mathers LP* [CD]. Interscope; Aftermath; Shady.
Eminem. (2000b). 'Kill You'. In: *The Marshall Mathers LP* [CD]. Interscope; Aftermath.
Eminem. (2000c). 'Stan'. In: *The Marshall Mathers LP* [CD]. Interscope; Aftermath.
Eminem. (2009). 'Insane'. In: *Relapse* [CD]. Interscope; Aftermath.
Eminem. (2013a). 'Bad Guy'. In: *The Marshall Mathers LP 2* [CD]. Interscope; Aftermath; Shady.
Eminem & Sasha Jenkins. (2009). *The Way I am*. New York: Plume Books.
Fender, S. (2024a). [@Sam_Fender]. https://www.instagram.com/reel/DCFPEkWtcbz/?igsh=YTJlZGxvNGtzYjVv (accessed 1 December 2024).
Fender, S. (2024b). 'People Watching'. https://www.youtube.com/watch?v=DHzaHMmXB6Y (accessed 1 December 2024).

REFERENCES

Felluga, D. F. (2003). 'Novel poetry: Transgressing the law of genre.' *Victorian Poetry*, 41(4), 490–499.

Foden, G. (2001). 'Just how good is he?' https://www.theguardian.com/books/2001/feb/06/poetry.features (accessed 27 April 2023).

Ford, A, & Heino, A. (2019). 'Don't dream it's over: Crowded House, The Beatles, and the making of a melody.' https://www.theguardian.com/music/2019/dec/01/dont-dream-its-over-crowded-house-the-beatles-and-the-making-of-a-melody (accessed 29 November 2024).

Fosbraey, G. (2015) [2017]. 'Disrupting Status Quo: Pedagogical Approaches to Song Lyrics.' In: *Creative Academic 2*.

Fosbraey, G. (2017). 'I'm (not) your man'. In: Billingham, P. (ed.) *Spirituality and Desire in Leonard Cohen's Songs and Poems: Visions from the Tower of Song*. United Kingdom: Cambridge Scholars Publishing.

Fosbraey, G. (2021). 'Featuring… Nicki Minaj'. In: Fosbraey, G. and Puckey (eds.). *Misogyny, Toxic Masculinity, and Heteronormativity in Post-2000 Popular Music*. London: Palgrave Macmillan.

Fosbraey, G. (2022a). *Viva Hate: exploring hatred in popular music*. London: Cambridge Scholars Press.

Fosbraey, G. (2022b). *Reading Eminem*. London: Palgrave Macmillan.

Fosbraey, G. (2022c). 'Manipulation and truth in The Final Cut.' In: Hart, C. and Morrison, S. (eds.). *The Routledge Handbook of Pink Floyd*. London: Routledge.

Fosbraey, G. (2022d). 'From Endless Summer to Endless Bummer: The Californian 'beach song' from 1962–2020'. In: Fosbraey, G (ed.) *Lost Horizons: Song Lyrics and the Coast*. London: Routledge.

Fosbraey, G. & Melrose, A. (2019). *Writing Song Lyrics: Creative and Critical Approaches*. Palgrave Macmillan.

Foucault, M. (1999). 'What is an author?' (J. V. Harari, Trans.). In Faubion, J. D. (ed.), *Aesthetics, Method, and Epistemology: Essential Works of Foucault, 1954–1984* (Vol. II, pp. 205–222). New York: The New Press.

Fox, K. (2004). *Watching The English: The Hidden Rules of English Behaviour*. London: Hodder & Stoughton.

Freund, E. (1987). *The Return of the Reader*. New York: Methuen.

Frisicks-Warren, B. (2006). *I'll Take You There: Pop Music and the Urge for Transcendence*. London: Continuum.

Frith, S. (1996). 'Music and identity.' *Questions of Cultural Identity*, 1(1), 108–128.

Frith, S. (1996). *Performing Rites*. Oxford: Oxford University Press.

Frith, S. (1998). *Performing rites: On the value of popular music*. Harvard University Press.

Frith, S. (ed.). (2004). *Popular Music: Critical Concepts in Media and Cultural Studies*. United Kingdom, Routledge.

Frith, S. Straw, W. & Street, J. (eds). (2001). *Pop and Rock*. Cambridge: Cambridge University Press.

Frith, S., & Horne, H. (2016). *Art into Pop*. London: Routledge..

Gans, H. (2010). *Popular Culture and High Culture: An Analysis and Evaluation of Taste Revised and Updated*. United States: Basic Books.

Garrigós, C. & Ahonen, M. (2023). *Women in Rock Memoirs: Music, History, and Life-Writing*. United States: Oxford University Press.

Genius (2016a). Eminem 'Verified Annotation' for 'Shady XV'. https://genius.com/Eminem-shadyxv-lyrics#about (accessed 25 April 2025).

Genius (2016b). Eminem 'Verified Annotation' for 'Criminal'. https://genius.com/artists/Eminem (accessed 25 April 2025).
Genius (2022). 'About Page'. https://genius.com/Genius-about-genius-annotated (accessed 25 April 2025).
Gentleman, A. (2010). 'Is Britain broken?' https://www.theguardian.com/society/2010/mar/31/is-britain-broken (accessed 1 December 2024).
Geoghegan, K. (2013). 'Lou Reed: In his own words'. https://www.bbc.co.uk/news/entertainment-arts-24704260 (accessed 1 December 2024).
Giles, J. & Middleton, T. (eds.). (1995). *Writing Englishness 1900–1950*. London: Routledge.
Goldstein, R. (1969). *Poetry of Rock*. New York: Bantam.
Gottlieb, R. and Kimbal, R. (eds.) (2000). *Reading Lyrics*. New York: Pantheon Books.
GOV.UK. (2015a). 'Policy paper. 2010 to 2015 government policy: sustainable development'. https://www.gov.uk/government/publications/2010-to-2015-government-policy-sustainable-development/2010-to-2015-government-policy-sustainable-development (accessed 6 December 2024).
GOV.UK. (2015b). 'Policy paper 2010 to 2015 government policy: house building'. https://www.gov.uk/government/publications/2010-to-2015-government-policy-house-building/2010-to-2015-government-policy-house-building development (accessed 6 December 2024).
Green, T. H. (2010). 'Q&A Special: Musician Ben Drew, aka Plan B'. https://theartsdesk.com/new-music/qa-special-musician-ben-drew-aka-plan-b (accessed 3 December 2024).
Greenblatt, S. (1995). "Culture." Critical Terms for Literary Study. In Tyson, L. (2006) Critical Theory Today. 2nd ed. New York: Routledge.
Grieg, F. (2018). '35 of Morrissey's most controversial quotes'. https://inews.co.uk/culture/morrisseys-most-controversial-quotes- (accessed 7 December 2024).
Gunderson, E. (2009). *The Cambridge Companion to Ancient Rhetoric*. Spain: Cambridge University Press.
Gutowitz, J. (2020). 'What Is Every Song on Taylor Swift's folklore Actually About?' https://www.vulture.com/2020/07/taylor-swift-every-folklore-song-explained.html (accessed 30 November 2024).
Happy Hippies. (2024). 'Who we are'. https://www.happyhippies.org/ (accessed 30 November 2024).
Harrison, E. (2023). 'Taylor Swift is a real poet, Shakespeare expert says, as he compares here to the Bard.' https://www.independent.co.uk/arts-entertainment/music/news/taylor-swift-shakespeare-lyrics-b2320716.html (accessed 22 April 2023).
Hattenstone, S. (2023). "I'm a CBE, I'm poet laureate so I'm clearly not a republican am I?': Simon Armitage on his radical roots and rock star dreams'. https://www.theguardian.com/books/2023/apr/08/simon-armitage-poet-laureate-radical-roots-rock-star-dreams (accessed 15 May 2023).
Hargreaves, D.J. & North, A. C. (eds.) (1997). *The social psychology of music*. Oxford: Oxford University Press.
Haven, K. (1999). *Creative Writing using storytelling techniques*. Colorado: Teachers Ideas Press.
Hayton, R. (2012). 'Fixing Broken Britain'. In: Heppell, T., & Seawright, D. (eds.). *Cameron and the Conservatives*. London: Palgrave Macmillan. https://doi.org/10.1057/9780230367487_10.

REFERENCES

HDK (2024). 'Social media: 5 tips digital marketers can learn from Taylor Swift's strategy'. https://www.culturehive.co.uk/resources/social-media-5-tips-digital-marketers-can-learn-from-taylor-swifts-strategy/ (accessed 8 December 2024).

Helm, T. & Asthana, A. (2010). 'Tuition fees rise is 'act of vandalism' says Ed Miliband'. https://www.theguardian.com/society/2010/dec/04/ed-miliband-student-fees-vandalism (accessed 21 September 2024).

Herman, D. (2009). *Basic Elements of Narrative*. Oxford: Wiley-Blackwell.

Hesmondhalgh, D. & Negus, K. (eds.). (2002) *Popular Music Studies*. New York: Arnold.

Hill, T. (2012). *Fifty years with The Beatles*. Hertfordshire: Atlantic World.

Hirwani, P. (2023). 'Jesy Nelson recalls last time she spoke to former Little Mix bandmates'. https://www.independent.co.uk/arts-entertainment/music/news/jesy-nelson-little-mix-two-years-b2321633.html (accessed 21 September 2024).

Hodges, D. A. & Sebald, D. C. (2011). *Music in the Human Experience*. Basingstoke: Routledge.

Hogan, 2010. 'Time Flies: Oasis'. https://pitchfork.com/reviews/albums/14392-time-flies/ (accessed 21 September 2023).

Holub, R. C. (1984). *Reception Theory*. New York: Methuen.

Hoover, A. (2016). *Bob Dylan lyrics as literature: First songwriter to win a Nobel Prize*. Christian Science Monitor. https://link.gale.com/apps/doc/A466506914/STND?u=ucwinch&sid=bookmark-STND&xid=6296a4d7 (accessed 27 April 2023).

Hodges, D. A. & Sebald, D. C. (2011). *Music in the Human Experience*. London: Routledge.

Hopps, G. (2009). *The Pageant of His Bleeding Heart*. London: Continuum.

Horner, B. & Swiss, T. (1999). *Key Terms in Popular Music and Culture*. Oxford: Blackwell.

Horsdal, M. (2012). *Telling Lives: Exploring Dimensions of narratives*. Abingdon: Routledge.

Hull, G. P., Hutchison, T. W., Strasser, R. (2011). *The Music Business and Recording Industry: Delivering Music in the 21st Century*. United Kingdom: Routledge.

Hurrey, A. (2013). 'Where's the Talking?' A guide to the language of Sunday League football'. https://www.theguardian.com/sport/football-cliches/2013/oct/31/talking-language-sunday-league-football (accessed 25 July 2021).

Ingate, M. (2024). "Heroin': The Velvet Underground's ode to William S Burroughs?' https://faroutmagazine.co.uk/the-velvet-undergrounds-ode-to-william-s-burroughs/ (accessed 1 December 2024).

Inglis, I. (ed). (2000) *The Beatles, Popular Music and Society*. Basingstoke: Macmillan.

Inglis, S. (2003). *Neil Young's Harvest*. United Kingdom: Bloomsbury Academic.

Iqani, M. (2012). *Consumer Culture and the Media: Magazines in the public eye*. Basingstoke: Palgrave Macmillan.

Jenal, C. (2021). *Modern Approaches to the Visualization of Landscapes*. Germany: VS VERLAG FUR SOZIALWISSE.

Johnson, B. (2013). 'Eminem Finally Apologizes to Mom on 'Headlights'. https://www.rollingstone.com/music/music-news/eminem-finally-apologizes-to-mom-on-headlights-248931/ (accessed 14 July 2021).

Johnson, B. (2019). 'Cancel Morrissey? – controversy over music and free speech'. https://www.opendemocracy.net/en/countering-radical-right/cancel-morrissey-controversy-over-music-and-free-speech/ (accessed 7 December 2024).

Johnson, M. (2009). *Pop Music Theory* (2nd edition). Boston: Cinemasonique Music.

Jones, O. (2012). Chavs: The Demonization of the Working Class. London: Verso.

Jones, R. E. & Davies, E. (2017). *Under my Thumb: Songs that hate women and the women who love them*. London: Repeater Books.

Jowett, G. S., & O'Donnell, V. (2015). *Propaganda & Persuasion* (6th edition). Los Angeles: Sage.
Juslin, P. N. & Sloboda, J. A. (2001). *Music and emotion*. Oxford: Oxford University Press.
Kelly, D. B. (2020). 'Insane Times Music Artists Were Screwed Over By Their Recording Companies'. https://www.grunge.com/227415/insane-times-music-artists-were-screwed-over-by-their-recording-companies/ (accessed 30 November 2024).
Kemp, A. (1997). 'Individual differences in musical behaviour'. In: Hargreaves, D.J. & North, A.C. (eds). (1997). *The Social Psychology of Music*. Oxford: Oxford University Press.
Kim, E. (2024). 'Photography Composition: Which Direction is Your Subject Looking?' https://erickimphotography.com/blog/2018/08/29/photography-composition-which-direction-is-your-subject-looking/ (accessed 10 December 2024).
Kimont, K. (2024). 'The Meaning Behind Charli XCX's Mega Viral Song "Apple"'. https://www.nbc.com/nbc-insider/charli-xcx-apple-lyrics-meaning-about (accessed 30 November 2024).
King, S. (2001). *On Writing*. London: Hodder & Stoughton.
Kirsch, S. (2014). *Gertrude Stein and the Reinvention of Rhetoric*. United States: University of Alabama Press.
Klein, M. (2005). *Intertextuality in Western Art Music*. Indiana: Indiana University Press.
Knowles, J. (Director). (1996). *Farewell to the World* [Film]. Polygram Video.
Kruger, D. (2008). 'I wrote 'hug a hoodie' and I'm proud of it'. https://www.spectator.co.uk/article/i-wrote-hug-a-hoodie-and-i-m-proud-of-it/ (accessed 5 December 2024).
Kunow, Rüdiger & Mussil, Stephan (eds.). (2013). *Text or Context. Reflections on Literary and Cultural Criticism*. Würzburg: Königshausen & Neumann.
Lamarque, P., & Olsen, S. (1996). *Truth, Fiction, and Literature: A Philosophical Perspective*. Oxford : Oxford University Press.
Lawrence, T. (2012). 'Global praise for 'superb' London 2012 Olympics'. https://www.independent.co.uk/news/uk/home-news/global-praise-for-superb-london-2012-olympics-8037820.html (accessed 3 December 2024).
Lee, M. (2005). *Writers on Writing: The Art of the Short Story*. Westport: Praeger.
Leith, S. (2007). 'Bob Dylan is a genius, but he's no poet'. http://www.telegraph.co.uk/comment/personal-view/3642416/Bob-Dylan-is-a-genius-but-hes-no-poet.html (accessed 12 August, 2024).
Leith, S. (2012). *You Talking to Me?* London: Profile Books.
Levitin, D. (2008a). *This is Your Brain on Music*. London: Atlantic Books.
Levitin, D. (2008b). *The World in Six Songs*. London: Aurum.
Lewis, C. (2013). 'Rich People Who Pretend to Be Poor Are Obnoxious'. https://www.vice.com/en/article/rich-people-who-pretend-to-be-poor-are-obnoxious/ (accessed 12 August 2024).
Lewisohn, M. (2013). *The Beatles – All These Years: Volume One: Tune In*. United Kingdom: Little, Brown Book Group.
Lockwood, R. (1996). *The Reader's Figure: Epideictic Rhetoric in Plato, Aristotle, Bossuet, Racine and Pascal*. Switzerland: Librairie Droz.
Longdon, V. (2018). 'Why are pop songs 3 minutes long?' https://www.classicfm.com/discover-music/why-are-pop-songs-3-minutes/ (accessed 19 August 2024).
Longhurst, B. (2007). *Popular Music and Society*. United Kingdom: Wiley.

REFERENCES

Lott, T. (2013). 'I've left my working-class roots behind. So why does Radio 4 still annoy me?' https://www.independent.co.uk/voices/comment/i-ve-left-my-workingclass-roots-behind-so-why-does-radio-4-still-annoy-me-8815130.html (accessed 3 December 2024).

Lynn, S. (1994). *Text and Contexts: Writing about Literature with Critical Theory*. New York: Harper Collins College Publishers.

Machor, J. L. & Goldstein, P. (2001). *Reception Study*. Abingdon: Routledge.

Maini (2024). 'Capturing Emotions – Sadness & Despair'. https://cottages.live/2021/04/10/capturing-emotions-sadness-despair/ (accessed 10 December 2024).

Marshall, P. D. (2014). *Celebrity and Power: Fame in Contemporary Culture*. United States: University of Minnesota Press.

Maxim (2009). 'Rated: 24 hours to live'. *February 2009 edition*.

McCaw, N. (2008). *How to read texts*. London: Continuum.

McCaw, N. (2013). *How to Read Texts: A Student Guide to Critical Approaches and Skills*, 2nd Edition. United Kingdom: Bloomsbury Academic.

McCloskey, D. N. (1994). *Knowledge and Persuasion in Economics*. United Kingdom: Cambridge University Press.

McDonald, R. (2007). *The Death of the Critic*. London: Continuum.

McDonald, R., Hargreaves, D. & Miell, D. (eds). (2002). *Musical Identities*. Oxford: Oxford University Press.

McKee, R. (1999). *Story*. London: Methuen.

McQuillan, M. (ed.) (2000). *The Narrative Reader*. London: Routledge.

Mesiti, P. (1993). *It's Only Rock 'n' Roll But-*. Australia: ANZEA.

Mocini, R. (2005). 'The verbal discourse of tourist brochures.' *Annals*, 5, 153–162.

Mojo (2023). 'Crowded House Interviewed'. https://www.mojo4music.com/articles/stories/crowded-house-interviewed/ (accessed 29 November 2024).

Montgomery, C. & Moore, E. (2018). *Language and a Sense of Place: Studies in Language and Region*. United Kingdom: Cambridge University Press.

Montgomery, M., Durant, A., Furniss, T., Mills, S. (2013). *Ways of Reading*. London: Routledge.

Moore, A. (2002). 'Authenticity as Authentication'. *Popular Music* 21(2). 214–220.

Moore, A. (2003). [Review of Popular Music Studies, by D. Hesmondhalgh & K. Negus]. *Popular Music*, 22(3), 386–390. http://www.jstor.org/stable/3877586.

Mosher, H. F. (1989). 'The Lyrics of American Music: A New Poetry'. In: Scheurer, T.E. *American Popular Music: The age of rock*. United States: Bowling Green University Popular Press.

Musical U. (2024). 'Anatomy of a Song: The Three Most Common Song Forms'. https://www.musical-u.com/learn/anatomy-of-a-song-the-three-most-common-song-forms/ (accessed 17 July 2024).

Mylrea, H. (2023). 'Rita Ora 'You and I' review: pop giant plays it safe on diary-influenced third album'. https://www.rollingstone.co.uk/music/album-reviews/rita-ora-you-and-i-review-pop-giant-plays-it-safe-31144/ (accessed 17 July 2023).

Negus, K. (2012). Narrative, Interpretation, and the Popular Song. *The Musical Quarterly*, 95(2/3), 368–395. http://www.jstor.org/stable/41811631.

NME. (2012). Nicki Minaj: 'I won't be poor ever again'. 'https://www.nme.com/news/music/nicki-minaj-113-1276771 (accessed 3 July 2023).

Norman, P. (2004). *Shout! The True Story of the Beatles*. London: Pan Books.

NYFA. (2023). 'Point of View in Photography: 4 Examples'. https://www.nyfa.edu/student-resources/point-view-photography/ (accessed 9 December 2024).

Official Charts Company (2018). 'How the Official Charts are compiled'. https://www.officialcharts.com/getting-into-the-charts/how-the-charts-are-compiled/ (accessed 25 April 2025).

O'Hagan, S. (2003). 'Tangled Up In Bob'. https://www.theguardian.com/theobserver/2003/sep/14/music (accessed 3 April 2023).

Oliva, R., Bidarra, J. & Araúj, D. (2010). 'Video and storytelling in a digital world: interactions and narratives in videoclips'. In: *Comunicação e Sociedade*, vol. 32, 2017, pp. 459–476.

Ora, R, (2023). 'Shape of you'. In: *You and I* [Spotify]. BMG.

Orejuela, F. (2015). *Rap and Hip Hop Culture*. Oxford: Oxford University Press.

Oware, M. (2018). *I Got Something to Say*. Greencastle: Palgrave Macmillan.

Palmer, A. (2012). Bad Manors: Plan B reveals all about the ghetto violence that inspired his music and movie career. https://www.mirror.co.uk/3am/celebrity-news/ill-manors-director-plan-b-867019 (accessed 3 December 2024).

Parker, P. (1999). *The Art and Science of Screenwriting* (2nd edition). Exeter: Intellect Books.

Partridge, C. (2015). *Mortality and Music*. London: Bloomsbury.

Pasco, A. H. (2002) *Allusion: A Literary Graft*. Charlottesville: Rookwood Press.

Peddie, I. (ed). (2006). *The Resisting Muse: Popular Music and Social Protest*. Aldershot: Ashgate.

Plan B. (2012). 'iLL MANORS'. CD single. 679; Atlantic.

Plant, I. (2020). 'Using Your Subject's Eyes Creatively in Photography'. https://www.photomasters.com/post/using-your-subject-s-eyes-creatively-in-photography (accessed 10 December 2024).

Powell, J. (2010). *How Music Works*. London: Penguin.

PopMatters Staff. (2005). 'Eels: Blinking Lights and Other Revelations'. https://www.popmatters.com/eels-blinking-2495892823.html (accessed 26 November 2024).

Präkel, D. (2008). *Basics Photography 06: Working in Black & White*. Switzerland: Bloomsbury Academic.

Pritchard, T. (2015). '16 Songs That Don't Mean What You Think They Mean'. https://www.buzzfeed.com/tahliapritchard/weird-song-meanings (accessed 26 November 2024).

Rachel, D. (2013). *Isle of Noises*. London: Picador.

Railton, D. & Watson, P. (2011). *Music Video and the Politics of Representation*. Edinburgh: Edinburgh University Press.

Randall, M. (2024). 'You Suffer, by Napalm Death'. https://www.stereostories.com/you-suffer-by-napalm-death-story-by-mickey-randall/ (accessed 26 November 2024).

Rapaport, H. (2011). *The Literary Theory Toolkit*. Chichester: Blackwell.

Renfro, Y. (2023). 'What to do with beautiful art from wicked artists?' https://www.washingtonindependentreviewofbooks.com/index.php/bookreview/monsters-a-fans-dilemma (accessed 18 July 2023).

Ricks, C. (2004). *Dylan's Visions of Sin*. United Kingdom: Canongate Books.

Ricks, C. (2011). 'Christopher Ricks on The Poetry of Bob Dylan.' https://www.youtube.com/watch?v=DDS1YJsfvio (accessed 26 April 2023).

Roberts, R. (2019). 'Morrissey is anti-immigrant and backs a white nationalist political party. Why don't fans care?' https://www.latimes.com/entertainment-arts/music/story/2019-10-24/morrissey-anti-immigrant-white-nationalist-hollywood-bowl (accessed 8 December 2024).

Roberts, W. R. (1995). 'Rhetoric'. In: Barnes, J. ed. (1995). *The Complete works of Aristotle, The Revised Oxford Translation*. Princeton: Princeton University Press.

Rodman, G. B. (2006) 'Race... and Other Four Letter Words: Eminem and the Cultural Politics of Authenticity'. *Popular Communication*, 4(2), 95–121, DOI: 10.1207/s15405710pc0402_3.

Rojek, C. (2011). *Pop Music, Pop Culture*. United Kingdom: Wiley.

Rooksby, R. (2006). *Lyrics: Writing better words for your songs*. Milwaukee: Backbeat Books.

Rose, G. (2007). *Visual methodologies*. India: SAGE Publication.

Rose, T. (2008). *The Hip Hop Wars*. New York: Basic Books.

Rowse, D. (2024). 'Where is Your Subject Looking and Why Does it Matter?' https://digital-photography-school.com/where-is-your-subject-looking-and-why-does-it-matter/ (accessed 10 December 2024).

Rubin, M. & Aaron, C. (1999). 'Hot-tub orgies & kung fu breakdowns: a short history of the hip-hop skit.' *Spin*. March 1999 edition.

Ryan, K. (2023). 'The longest song ever was almost 6 days long'. https://entertainment.howstuffworks.com/longest-song-ever (accessed 29 November 2024).

Sanders, S. (2022). 'Nicki Minaj Praises Lil' Kim As An Influential Fashion Figure; Opens Up About Getting Booty Shots'. https://hellobeautiful.com/3584052/nicki-minaj-lil-kim-fashion/ (accessed 10 March 2023).

Savage, J. (2023). 'Brian Epstein: the brilliant but troubled man behind the Beatles'. https://www.historyextra.com/period/20th-century/brian-epstein-beatles-manager/ (accessed 28 November 2024).

Sawyer, M. (2011). 'Plan B: "Listen to my music. I'll help you through"'. https://www.theguardian.com/music/2011/jun/26/plan-b-listen-to-my-music (accessed 3 December 2024).

Schiller, M. (2018). 'Transmedia Storytelling: New Practices and Audiences'. In Christie I. & Van den Oever A. (eds.), *Stories* (pp. 97–108). Amsterdam: Amsterdam University Press. Doi: 10.2307/j.ctv5rf6vf.10.

Searle, J. R., Vanderveken, D. (1985). *Foundations of Illocutionary Logic*. United Kingdom: Cambridge University Press.

Selden, R., Widdowson, P.; Brooker, P. (2005). *A Reader's Guide to Contemporary Literary Theory* (5th edition) Edinburgh: Pearson's Education.

Self, W. (2011). 'The King of Bedsit Angst Grows Up'. In: Woods, P.A. (ed.). *Morrissey in Conversation*. London: Plexus.

Service, T. (2016). 'War music: the humanity, heroism and propaganda behind Shostakovich's Symphony No 7'. https://www.theguardian.com/music/2016/jan/02/war-music-the-humanity-heroism-and-propaganda-behind-shostakovich-symphony-no-7 (accessed 4 December 2024).

Shabo, M. (2010). *Rhetoric, Logic, and Argumentation: A Guide for Student Writers*. Clayton: Prestwick House, Inc.

Sheriff, J. K. (1989). *The Fate of Meaning: Charles Peirce, Structuralism, and Literature*. Princeton: Princeton University Press.

Shepherd, J. (ed). (2003). *Continuum Encyclopedia of Popular Music of the World, Volume 1: Media, Industry, Society*. Germany: Bloomsbury Academic.

Shuker, R. (1997). *Understanding Popular Music*. Basingstoke: Routledge.

Shuker, R. (2016). *Understanding Popular Music Culture*. United Kingdom: Taylor & Francis.

Siang, T. Y. (2022). 'The Key Elements & Principles of Visual Design'. https://www.interaction-design.org/literature/article/the-building-blocks-of-visual-design (accessed 20 November 2024).

Sigala, E. E. & Trainor, M. F. French Montana. (2018). 'Just Got Paid'. https://www.youtube.com/watch?v=HUJGwSy0pRI (accessed 20 November 2024).
Simkin, S. (2020). *What Makes the Monkey Dance: The Life and Times of Chuck Prophet and Green On Red*. London: Jawbone Press.
Simon, P. (2011). *Paul Simon: Lyrics 1964–2011*. New York: Simon & Schuster.
Simpson, D. (2005). 'Eels, Blinking Lights and Other Revelations'. https://www.theguardian.com/music/2005/apr/22/ (accessed 20 September 2024).
Sinfield, A. (1977). *Dramatic Monologue*. London: Methuen.
Skinner, M. (2012). *The Story of The Streets*. London: Corgi Books.
Sloan, N, & Harding, C. (2020) *Switched on Pop: How Popular Music works, and why it matters*. Oxford: Oxford University Press.
Song Exploder Podcast (2016). 'Weezer – Summer Elaine and Drunk Dory'. Available at: http://songexploder.net/weezer (accessed 11 August 2024).
Sontag, S. (1977). *On Photography*. New York: Farrar, Straus and Giroux.
Starkey, G. (2004). *Radio in Context*. London: Palgrave MacMillan.
Stay Free Radio (2024). 'Charli XCX Apple Meaning and Review'. https://www.stayfreeradioip.com/post/charli-xcx-apple-meaning-and-review (accessed 1 December 2024).
Street, J. (2013). *Music and Politics*. United Kingdom: John Wiley & Sons.
Stringfellow, F. (1994). *The Meaning of Irony: A Psychoanalytic Investigation*. Albany: State University of New York Press.
Stubbs, D. (2019). 'Why It's Time To Ditch Your Morrissey-Loving Friend'. https://thequietus.com/opinion-and-essays/black-sky-thinking/morrissey-racism-fans-idiots/ (accessed 1 December 2024).
Tambling, J. (1991). *Narrative and Ideology*. Buckingham: Open University Press.
Taylor, D. (2014). *Understanding Composition*. East Sussex: Ammonite Press.
Taylor, S. (2019). 'Stan — how Eminem's hit from 2000 gave rise to today's stan culture' https://ig.ft.com/life-of-a-song/stan.html (accessed 13 April 2023).
Taylor, T. (2000) [2007]. 'His Name was in Lights: Chuck Berry's 'Johnny B. Goode'. In: Middleton, R. (ed.). *Reading Pop*. Oxford: Oxford University Press.
The Beatles (2000). *Anthology*. London: Cassell & Co.
Thomson, G. (2008). *I Shot a Man in Reno*. London: Continuum.
Thompson, T. (1967). 'Interview for Life Magazine. Friday, June 16, 1967'.https://www.the-paulmccartney-project.com/interview/interview-for-life-magazine/ (accessed 21 November 2023).
Tiwary, V. (2014). 'Brian Epstein: The Fifth Beatle'. https://www.cbsnews.com/newyork/news/brian-epstein-the-man-who-brought-us-the-beatles/ (accessed 21 November 2024).
Truby, J. (2008). *The Anatomy of Story: 22 Steps to Becoming a Master Storyteller*. United States: Farrar, Straus and Giroux.
UK Parliament. (2024). 'General Election 2010: key issues for the 2010 Parliament'. https://www.parliament.uk/business/publications/research/key-issues-for-the-new-parliament/the-new-parliament/general-election/ (accessed 22 November 2024).
Vallely, P. (2012). 'Paul Vallely: Hating chavs is also a form of prejudice'. https://www.independent.co.uk/voices/commentators/paul-vallely-hating-chavs-is-also-a-form-of-prejudice-6286634.html (accessed 3 December 2024).
Vernallis, C. (2004). *Experiencing Music Video: Aesthetics and Cultural Context*. New York: Columbia University Press.

REFERENCES

VH1. (2000). 'THE MARSHALL MATHERS LP'. http://www.vh1.com/shows/series/ultimate_albums/marshall/interview_eminem.jhtml (accessed 9 December 2024).

Vos, T. (2018). *Journalism*. Germany: De Gruyter.

Wainwright, O. (2022). "A massive betrayal': how London's Olympic legacy was sold out.' https://www.theguardian.com/uk-news/2022/jun/30/a-massive-betrayal-how-londons-olympic-legacy-was-sold-out (accessed 22 November 2024).

Walker, P. (2019). 'Was Boris Johnson as successful as London mayor as he claims?' https://www.theguardian.com/politics/2019/jun/12/was-boris-johnson-as-successful-as-london-mayor-as-he-claims (accessed 25 April 2025).

Wardle, D. (2012). 'How The Beatles cracked America: The Ed Sullivan Show.' https://faroutmagazine.co.uk/how-the-beatles-cracked-america-the-ed-sullivan-show/ (accessed 22 November 2024).

Way, L. C. S. & McKerrell, S. (2017). *Music as Multimodal Discourse: Semiotics, Power and Protest*. United Kingdom: Bloomsbury Publishing.

Webb, J. (1998). *Tunesmith*. New York: Hyperion.

Weber, E. T. (2016). *The Beatles and the Historians*. North Carolina: McFarland & Company.

Weigand, E. (2008). *Dialogue and Rhetoric*. Netherlands: John Benjamins.

Weingarten, C. (2013). 'Eminem Nerds Out, Turns Up, And Raps His Ass Off On 'The Marshall Mathers LP 2'. https://www.spin.com/2013/11/eminem-the-marshall-mathers-lp-2-kendrick-lamar-rick-rubin/ (accessed 14 April 2023).

Westhoff, B. (2017). *Original Gangstas*. New York: Hachette.

Weyandt, D. (2013). 'Drink your own bathwater'. https://www.urbandictionary.com/define.php?term=drink%20your%20own%20bathwater (accessed 22 November 2024).

Willett, A. (2013). *Media Production: A Practical Guide to Radio & TV*. United Kingdom: Taylor & Francis.

Wodak, R. & Krzyzanowski, M. (eds.) (2008). *Qualitative Discourse Analysis in the Social Sciences*. Basingstoke: Palgrave Macmillan.

Wyatt, D. (2013). 'Robin Thicke's number one single 'Blurred Lines' accused of reinforcing rape myths'. https://www.independent.co.uk/arts-entertainment/music/news/robin-thicke-s-number-one-single-blurred-lines-accused-of-reinforcing-rape-myths-8667199.html (accessed 1 December 2024).

Yang, Q. (2016). 'Music Video Breakdown: 'Shout Out to My Ex' by Little Mix'. https://www.thecrimson.com/article/2016/11/1/mvv-shout-out/ (accessed 14 April 2024).

Zimmerman, B. (2005). *Edgar Allan Poe: Rhetoric and Style*. Ithaca: McGill-Queen's University Press.

Zollo, P. (2003). *Songwriters on Songwriting*, (4th edition). Ohio: Da Capo Press.

Zuckerkandl, V. (1973). 'The Meaning of Song', in Clayton, M. (ed.) (2008). *Music, Words and Voice: A Reader*. Manchester: Manchester University Press.

www.ingramcontent.com/pod-product-compliance
Lightning Source LLC
Chambersburg PA
CBHW030143170426
43199CB00008B/187